Every Tribe and Tongue

Every Tribe and Tongue

A Biblical Vision for Language in Society

MICHAEL PASQUALE
NATHAN L. K. BIERMA

☙PICKWICK *Publications* · Eugene, Oregon

EVERY TRIBE AND TONGUE
A Biblical Vision for Language in Society

Copyright © 2011 Michael Pasquale and Nathan L. K. Bierma. All rights reserved. Except for brief quotations in critical publications or reviews, no part of this book may be reproduced in any manner without prior written permission from the publisher. Write: Permissions, Wipf and Stock Publishers, 199 W. 8th Ave., Suite 3, Eugene, OR 97401.

Pickwick Publications
An Imprint of Wipf and Stock Publishers
199 W. 8th Ave., Suite 3
Eugene, OR 97401

www.wipfandstock.com

ISBN 13: 978-1-60899-014-6

Cataloguing-in-Publication data:

Pasquale, Michael.

    Every tribe and tongue : a biblical vision for language in society / Michael Pasquale and Nathan L. K. Bierma.

    xii + 84 pp. ; 23 cm. Includes bibliographical references.

    ISBN 13: 978-1-60899-014-6

    1. Language and languages—Religious aspects—Christianity. 2. Christianity and culture. I. Bierma, Nathan L. K. II. Title.

BR115.C8 .P37 2011

Manufactured in the U.S.A.

Contents

Acknowledgments / vii
Introduction / ix

1. Speaking Beauty into the Chaos / 1
2. Pentecost in Practice: The Call to Linguistic Diversity / 10
3. Love Your Neighbor: The Ethics of Hospitality / 17
4. From Every Nation: Immigration and Language / 24
5. Teach Your Children Well: Language in Education / 39
6. The Word of the Lord: The Language of Scripture and Worship / 47
7. Language Purity and Language Play: Beauty in Variety / 62
8. Go Into All the World: Transformed Linguistic Communities / 73

Bibliography / 81

Acknowledgments

We would like to thank the many people who helped shape this project and bring it to fruition.

Thanks to Jim Tedrick, Christian Amondson, and Charlie Collier of Wipf and Stock Publishers for their editorial guidance and help in making the book a reality.

Thanks to those who offered insight and comments on our book from the proposal stage to final drafts. We thank Tom Scovel, Joan Dungey, Laura Hahn, Gena Bennett, Karen Asenavage, Wes Eby, Bill Commons, Jan Dormer, David Sims, Jim Vanden Bosch, Karen Miller, and Michael Stevens for their feedback and encouragement.

Thanks also to the folks at the Civitas Center at Cornerstone University and the Calvin Center for Christian Scholarship Linguistics Reading group who helped shape our thoughts on the issues presented in the book. Collegiality and collaboration were at the heart of this project.

Collaboration on any project brings its challenges and blessings, however this book was definitely strengthened through this joint effort. Many thanks to Nathan for his diligence in sharing his passion of a truly biblical vision of language and society, it has been a privilege working on this project with a fellow lover of words! Nathan lent his writing expertise to crafting chapters 1, 2, 6, and 7. I (Michael) shaped chapters 3, 4, 5, and 8. However, from those initial drafts we worked to develop a unity to the book and our words and thoughts can be found throughout. Special thanks also to Monica Pasquale and Michael Stevens who read through the final drafts meticulously and offered further points to clarify and strengthen our arguments.

We would like to thank our families for their love and support. Nathan thanks his wife Andrea and son Benjamin. Michael thanks his wife Monica and sons Alex and Daniel. We are thankful for wives and children who encourage and inspire us!

Acknowledgments

Many of the original ideas developed in this book came from classes that we have taught. This is especially the case for Michael's courses in *Sociolinguistics* and *Issues in TESOL* at Cornerstone University. Thanks so much to our students who have also contributed to our understanding of these topics. We dedicate this book to our students at Calvin College and Cornerstone University.

Introduction

Why Don't They All Just Speak English?

That was the question a woman asked Michael in church recently. He was giving a presentation in a church about teaching English as a Second Language (ESL) as a ministry, a way to reach out to the neighboring community that was predominantly Hispanic. He explained that an ESL ministry could build bridges into the community in order to minister to their needs. Then he said that it would also be great for the church to have "Spanish as a Second Language" classes so that the English congregation could reach out to Spanish speakers in their own language. The response he received from one church member caught him a bit off guard. During the question-and-answer time she challenged him as to why the church should not just "teach them all English" since "they are here in the U.S." The idea of using Spanish was out of the question; in her mind it was only logical or right to use English in that church.

Why don't they all just speak English? The question reverberates throughout the United States, publicly shouted or quietly wondered. Americans who struggle to understand the server at the fast food restaurant, the tech support person taking a customer service call in another country, or a bilingual sign at the doctor's office, may get frustrated by linguistic differences. Wouldn't it be easier if we all spoke the same language? Isn't refusing to speak English, or failing to speak it well, even a subtle form of disloyalty to America, a lack of solidarity with other Americans? Sometimes, no doubt, some of this frustration is tinged with racial prejudice. Other times, it may purely be irritation with miscommunication.

The pressing issue of Latin American immigration to the United States makes this kind of frustration more than just occasional and anecdotal. Americans hear and read about in the media and discuss with each other the ways the U.S. government is, and should be, responding to the waves of immigrants seeking to live in America—including those who bypass legal processes and enter the country as undocumented workers. Presidential races and congressional legislation puts questions of immigration front and center, and our leaders take an urgent interest in how we as citizens feel about these issues. Christian engagement in public discourse in America must address these issues head on and therefore cannot avoid these contentious debates.

The problem is, Christians tend to get very little guidance about how to respond to issues related to immigration—both the small-scale cross-cultural encounters at the fast food restaurant and the larger-scale political debate. Some churches boldly take political sides, other churches may try to distance themselves from all such controversy, but in neither case are they helping Christians to bring deeply biblical discernment to their public citizenship. Indeed, since the Bible apparently seems to say little, if anything, about these issues, some Christians might not see the need to make such a connection.

We offer this book as a way, first, to rediscover biblical stories and principles that relate to questions about immigration and societal multilingualism; and second, to outline possible ways to guide thoughtful engagement in the discourse of the "public square" based on this biblical witness. We will try to show that, far from being an afterthought in the Bible, the call to love our neighbors and to gather people of *every* nation in the worship of God is at the very core of the gospel message.

We write this book out of two powerful passions: first, a deeply-rooted love of God's gift of language to human beings, and second, a determination that the North American church take seriously its charge not simply to love the "stranger and alien" but to live as "strangers and aliens" within the American nation to which it has been called to witness.

We each love language and love linguistics—the academic study of language. However, we also each fear that when many American Christians enter public conversations about policies regarding language and immigration, they place their American national identity ahead of their kingdom citizenship. Tacitly or deliberately, American Christians often accept the assumptions that their own culture is the "norm" and other cultures are "different" (and the importance of this norm is surprisingly high in a land that prides itself on opportunity for all, in which most native-born citizens are only a few generations removed from their own ancestors' immigration).

We stress that we are not interested merely in a Christianized form of "political correctness." We welcome calls for "celebrating diversity" and "practicing tolerance" in America, but we refuse to leave it at that. We are not called to "tolerate" others, but to love and embrace others as neighbors, and thus as ourselves. And more profoundly, we are called to see *ourselves* "as aliens and strangers in the world" (1 Pet 2:11). Moses tells the Israelites in Deut 10:19, "You shall love the stranger, for you were strangers in the land of Egypt." Our treatment of the "strangers" among us must be deeply rooted in the reality that we, too, are strangers whom God has embraced as his own.

1

Speaking Beauty into the Chaos

God's creation began with language. "Then God said..." we read in Genesis 1. God *said*. And it happened; God said, "Let there be light," and there was light. Of all the ways God could have caused creation to happen, Scripture tells us that God, in some mysterious way, used *speech*.

Language, it seems from Scripture, is integral to the act of creation, and integral to who God is. God speaks, God acts, and creation bursts forth. God's word, and words, goes out into all creation, and creation becomes a beautiful echo of his good words.

God's word went out, Genesis says, over the "formless void and [the] darkness [that] covered the face of the deep." God's creative speech results in the opposite of chaos; creation turns chaos into order, formlessness into beauty, darkness into light. God's word thunders over the chaotic void, and creation blossoms. God creates by speaking beauty into the chaos.

From the beginning, then, God's word has brought the universe to order and goodness. Instead of a "formless void," there is a beautifully formed world. Instead of chaos, there is beauty—and all because "God said."

"By God's speech that which did not exist comes into being," writes Walter Brueggemann in his commentary on Genesis. "The way of God with his world is the way of language. God speaks something new that never was before."[1]

God created the world by his *dabar*, his word. The Hebrew word *dabar* can mean both "word" and "thing." The ambiguity suggests a connection, and there is one: God's *dabar* creates a *dabar*; his word creates a thing. We heard a rabbi recently say that he tries to remember this double

1. Brueggemann, *Genesis*, 24.

meaning as he looks around at God's world. "I see things in creation and try to think of them not as things, but as God's spoken words. I see a bird and I think, 'there's God's spoken word.'"

Then, as God's finishing touch on creation, God says, "let us make humankind in our image, according to our likeness," in order to help watch over the world. Not because God can't handle the job without humans, but because God delights in creating creatures who are stamped with his likeness. He walked with them, and he *talked* with them.

"It is not surprising that God, who is 'far beyond what we can ask or think' should deal with us by means of language," Eugene Peterson writes. "God speaks. For Christians, basic spirituality is not only a noun, *God*, but also a verb, *Said* (or *Says*)."[2]

And the first thing these image-bearers are asked to do is to speak. Speak words, speak truth, assign linguistic units and meaning to the reality of God's creation. "The Lord God formed every animal of the field and every bird of the air, and brought them to the man to see what he would call them; and whatever the man called each living creature, that was its name." The first body part human beings are on record as using is the tongue.

To this day, humans are called to speak beauty into the chaos. Where herds of unclassified animals roam or fly, humans speak order into the anonymity. Where our tongues would be tied for lack of a linguistic symbol to use, humans make a system of symbolic communication. Every name, every term, every vocabulary word and function word in every language ever used by humans, has been merely a continuation of this naming act that we were created for. "Just as Adam named the creatures in the Garden of Eden, we define ideas and objects by using vast vocabularies of verbal and nonverbal symbols that subtly represent (or misrepresent) the reality of God's world," says Quentin Schultze.[3]

God spoke beauty into the chaos, spoke humans into existence, and immediately seemed to say, "now keep it going." Keep speaking beauty into the chaos. "God created us to be stewards of symbolic reality," writes Schultze.[4] As Stephen Webb states:

---

2. Peterson, *Subversive Spirituality*, 23.
3. Schultze, *Communicating for Life*, 23.
4. Ibid., 21.

We can add our voices to the divine harmony because we were created in God's image. Theologically construed, speaking is not a trait projected upon God by analogy to human experience. We do not speak first and then think about God as speaking too. On the contrary, we can speak only because God created us to be hearers of God's Word. We are created in God's image, but that image is more like an echo than a mirror. God spoke us into being so that we too might have the joy of sharing in the spoken Word.[5]

God created us for language, but not for any one language. Rabbis used to muse that Hebrew was the perfect language, assuming that Adam and Eve spoke Hebrew in the Garden of Eden, and that Hebrew was the "one language" talked about in Genesis 11 before the Tower of Babel (for a different reading of this passage, see chapter 2). Hebrew was indeed used by God to speak with Israel, and its descendant, Aramaic, was used by Jesus during his life on earth. But beyond that, Hebrew is simply another language among languages. Any language can and does allow humans to employ their image-bearing linguistic ability. No language is better than any other at doing it. We should see language as a sacred gift from God, but should not see our native language, or your native language, or anyone's native language, as any more holy or blessed than any other. We will look at this more next chapter, but for now we can say: Language is a gift; *a* language is a tool.

Nor does this mean that a person must be able to speak in order to bear God's image, any more than it means someone must be able to see or walk in order to bear God's image, simply because that is how God created humans. All human beings bear the image of God. People with linguistic disabilities still communicate, still speak and proclaim (with hands, with faces, with machine devices), because humans are communicating beings, whatever their abilities. As James Vanden Bosch says, "Although language is a significant part of what it means to be human, it is not the essence of a person's value in God's eye, and therefore a Christian . . . must not undervalue humans who are without language or who experience language impairments or deficits."[6]

Whatever their language, abilities, or personalities, humans are communicating beings. But humans are not talking robots, emitting whatever signals the programmer commands them to make. Instead,

---

5. Webb, *Divine Voice*, 15.
6. Vanden Bosch, "Language Power, Language Play, and Promises to Keep."

these image-bearing creatures are given a choice—keep on speaking beauty into the chaos, or instead, speak chaos into the beauty. God let the fate of the world, the future of his creation project, hinge on the words that humans would say next.

SPEAKING CHAOS INTO THE BEAUTY

Randall Dale Adams was on trial for the 1976 murder of a Dallas police officer. Two witnesses said they saw Adams pull the trigger. A third, a psychologist, testified that Adams would remain a threat to society unless he was given the death penalty. Adams was found guilty and sentenced to death.

Adams' sentence was later commuted to life in prison on a technicality. But thirteen years later, the truth about the 1976 murder finally emerged: the two witnesses had lied in court. One of the witnesses, who had been released after he testified against Adams, probably committed the murder himself. That witness was later tried and executed for another murder.[7]

With our ability to use language, we have great capacity to speak beauty into the chaos. But because of the effects of sin, we often do just the opposite; we speak chaos into the beauty. We have the opportunity to use our language to echo the truth, clarity, and goodness to God's creation. But sin leads us to speak words that build lies, suspicion, pride, nationalism, and destruction in God's world.

God created the good world by speaking words; the serpent brought ruin to creation by speaking words of his own. "Eat the fruit from that tree and you will be like God," the serpent says to seduce Eve into sin. The words, and the actions they prompt, turn the beautiful garden into a house of lies.

Once the deceit and the defiant act it prompted has pumped chaos into the garden, the words and the lies keep flowing. "Did you eat that fruit?" God asks Adam, and he whimpers and says, "Eve—she made me do it." "Is that true?" God asks Eve, and she says, "The serpent made me do it." God asks direct questions, but the words pile up like sandbags, filled with denial, evasion, and blame.

Ever since, we humans have kept on piling up words that speak chaos into the beauty, and falsehood into the truth. "Our communication

---

7. "Randall Dale Adams," *Center on Wrongful Convictions*.

becomes a pervasive, destructive idolatry," writes Quentin Schultze. "We spread distorted, selfish, and manipulative information. We lie, defame, verbally abuse, and gossip."[8] Our false and self-serving words go out into creation, and wherever they go, they spread the misery of sin.

The book of James does not underestimate the huge messes that we can make with our tongues:

> The tongue is a small part of the body, but it makes great boasts. Consider what a great forest is set on fire by a small spark. The tongue also is a fire, a world of evil among the parts of the body. It corrupts the whole person, sets the whole course of one's life on fire, and is itself set on fire by hell. All kinds of animals, birds, reptiles and sea creatures are being tamed and have been tamed by human beings, but no one can tame the tongue. It is a restless evil, full of deadly poison. With the tongue we praise our Lord and Father, and with it we curse human beings, who have been made in God's likeness. (James 3:5–9 TNIV)

Just as the tongue of the serpent was enough to start a wildfire of chaos in the Garden of Eden; we each can start raging fires of lies and pride with our tongues, our language-shapers. The tongue can fling out words of beauty or chaos. Often it opts for chaos. Maybe this is why James says earlier, in chapter 1, that we should be "quick to listen, slow to speak."

The two witnesses against Randall Dale Adams created chaos with their tongues. They spoke false words that piled up to form an apparent mound of evidence that Adams had committed murder. The words of the psychologist who testified against Adams piled up to form a picture of Adams as a man who was unfit to live. The words filled that courtroom, filled the ears and minds of all who were listening, and after all the words had been spoken, a man was unjustly sentenced to death. The tongue was nearly an "on" switch for the electric chair.

Few of us, perhaps, will lie under oath in court, but we all seize on opportunities to speak chaos into the beauty every single day. A boast, a half-truth, an evil silence, an excuse, a rumor, an outright lie—any of these can come rolling off our tongues at any time, because of the power of sin in us. We also feel the wounds of false words that have been uttered to us, about us, behind us, around us, and we suffer the pain of these words. No matter what language you speak, the words of your language contain the potential to speak beauty or to speak chaos.

8. Schultze, *Communicating for Life*, 75–76.

Into a world that was created good, created by God's speaking beauty into chaos—into that world we now speak words of chaos every day, and the world groans under the weight of these words, groans—as Romans 8 says—to have the burden of these words lifted, and for beauty to re-emerge, to win out over chaos. What does the world need in order for that to happen?

SPEAKING BEAUTY AGAIN INTO THE CHAOS

In an unmistakable echo of Genesis 1 and its story of what happened "In the beginning," John 1 ties the work of creation to God's ultimate act of love: the Incarnation, when God took on human flesh. And the name of God's incarnate presence is, unforgettably, *Logos*, "the Word." Scholars have since made Hebrew translations of John, and the Hebrew word they use for *Logos* is *dabar*.

> And the Word [*Logos, Dabar*] became flesh and lived among us, and we have seen his glory, the glory as of a father's only son, full of grace and truth. . . . No one has ever seen God. It is God the only Son, who is close to the Father's heart, who has made him known.

In the beginning, God's word went out over the waters and birthed creation. Now God's "Word," God's *dabar*, is birthed into creation as a human being, Jesus Christ, a person who uses human language and human languages to teach, to pray, and to cry, "It is finished!"

Before, God's people were told to "hear" the word of the Lord, and "hear" meant not only to receive but to obey. When they failed, God asked, "are you really listening? Can you hear me?" The failure is not just moral, it is communicative—a crisis of blocking out the word of the Lord. God sends his prophets, who insist "hear the word of the Lord," but the people's ears are closed.

And so finally God sends his loudest message ever. He sends not just more words, but the Word. He no longer speaks through human leaders, he comes as a human leader to speak. And not just speak, also to "hear," to obey, his own words of the law. The Word comes not only to speak but to *act*, to heal, to love, to weep, to touch, to throw tables, to bleed. Jesus was the only person who ever perfectly kept God's commandments, and, paradoxically, the only one to be fully punished as though he didn't. He came not only with a new sermon to preach ("you have heard . . . but I tell you"), but also came to live that sermon out by example. The way he lived seemed to say, or to suggest, "This is what it looks like to hear the word of the Lord." This is beauty instead of chaos.

Of course, his own obedient living was not enough to make things right, to restore the dream of creation, to re-speak beauty into chaos. Christ came not just to try to resist the chaos to but to finish it off, to let beauty trump chaos for eternity. But re-establishing the beauty would happen in a descent into the darkest depths of chaos imaginable. In order to let chaos have its last, final, fullest gasp, before it collapsed into beauty for the rest of time. On the cross we see the apparent triumph of chaos, the apparent failure of God's greatest attempt to speak beauty. The Word, for three days, is silenced. Before beauty wins—or maybe *in order* for beauty to win—beauty is first pushed to the brink of oblivion. The Word speaks in a dying sigh.

Then, in resurrection, the Word comes thundering out of the tomb, beauty is spoken back into chaos, and the creation dream is not only alive but it is eternally validated. The greatest hope of the "formless void" is dashed by God's victorious Word. Jesus rises and greets his followers, and to prove to them it's not just their imaginations, the first thing he does is to speak to them. "Mary," he says, and Mary lunges for him in recognition. "Hi," he says to his disciples, and they embrace him ecstatically. He says a blessing over the meal with the travelers from the road to Emmaus to show that once again, the Word has become flesh.

Only through the Word could the dream of speaking beauty become eternal reality—speaking beauty throughout creation, as far as chaos can reach. Christ's redemption happened not only to restore human beings to dialogue with God—though it does, wonderfully, that too. Christ's redemption happened for nothing less than to recapture the creation dream in all its cosmic scope, to speak beauty once again into the chaos, light into the darkness, as far as the skies stretch, wherever fish swim, grass sways, and creatures crawl. "Through him God was pleased to reconcile to himself all things, whether on earth or in heaven, by making peace through the blood of his cross," Paul says in Colossians 1.

In creation, God speaks beauty into chaos. In the Garden of Eden, humans speak chaos into the beauty. In Christ, God speaks beauty back into the chaos, once again, once and for all. And beauty becomes the language that will never be silenced.

To be transformed in Christ, then, is to be restored to dialogue with God—back on speaking terms—and also to be brought back in to God's grand dream of speaking beauty back into the chaos. Every word we speak, everything we do, everywhere we go in creation is a chance to speak this same beauty, or more accurately, to have God speak beauty through us. Every conversation, every task, every hour of work or play, gives us a chance to join in God's new creation project of speaking beauty back into the chaos, and over the chaos forever.

Our words are like notes we play in a symphony, says Quentin Schultze. "We enter the stage of God's creation and make our music. When we play well, in tune with our gifts and God's score, the music is magnificent. We pour spiritual life into a luscious creation. . . . On the other hand, when we stubbornly write our own score, we orchestrate dissonance, destruction, and despair."[9]

We play well, we speak beauty, not only in the truthfulness of our speech, but in the joy and hope, the compassion and courage, of our speech. And not only our speech but our actions—our "hearing" of God's word, and our living like Jesus did when God's Word became flesh.

We can speak beauty through our truthful speech in courtrooms, our loving speech in a talk with a friend, our mending speech in a conversation with an enemy. And we can speak beauty by listening to others' speech, since speaking beauty happens only in dialogue.

"The fact is that *all* human communication depends on God's grace," says Schultze. "First, our Creator has established the physical laws of sound and sight that we need to communicate. Second, God goes a step further, creating situations in which we can spread *shalom* even with our imperfect talents. Third, our Creator grants each of us the gifts necessary to communicate. In all these ways, grace arrests entropy [chaos] and makes productive communication possible."[10]

Christ died for nothing less than for God's good, loving communication to be restored—between humans and God, and between humans and other humans. The Word became flesh so that God's image-bearers could once again join God in speaking beauty into the chaos, in speaking light into the darkness. In our speech, in our actions, in our love, in our courage, we speak either chaos or beauty, darkness or light, despair or hope. In our language in the broadest sense—our shared communication

---

9. Schultze, *Communicating for Life*, 150.
10. Ibid., 34.

to deepen our understanding of each other, God, and creation—we, day by day, word by word, action by action, keep speaking chaos, or, through Christ the redeemer, we start to speak beauty again.

2

Pentecost in Practice

The Call to Linguistic Diversity

One constant of world history is that, whenever multiple nations have spoken the same language, one of them probably conquered the others. Few nations will voluntarily abandon their native tongue unless forced to by invaders. They might try to add a language to their repertoire, as a second language, in order to expand their trade, or improve their schools. But they'll only change their first language when forced at the point of a sword.

Take that principle and apply it to the familiar story of the Tower of Babel. What would a whole world speaking the same language be evidence of? Who would be the most happy with that? Who would be least happy?

You don't always hear these questions when the story of Babel is told. Often the story is told as a tragic fall from a harmonious perfect world—almost a second Fall, after the Fall in Eden. Once upon a time, according to this telling, everyone spoke the same language and understood each other perfectly, and there was world peace. Then God intervened and introduced linguistic confusion, and the nations of the world have been duking it out ever since.

This is one possible reading of the story of Babel. It is probably the most popular one. But the conquest question gives us reason to take a second look.

BABEL: THE REST OF THE STORY

Before there was Alexander the Great, there was Ashurbanipal of Assyria, a bloodthirsty king who made it his mission to conquer the then-known world. He was a war-mongerer who staged lion killings as a great spectacle to show off his power. In case anyone missed the show, he had artisans craft stone carvings depicting the bloody events, many of which can be seen today in the British Museum.[1] He added this inscription to one:

> I, Ashurbanipal, King of the Universe, king of Assyria, in my lordly sport. They let a fierce lion of the plain out of his cage and on foot . . . I stabbed him later with my iron girdle dagger and he died.[2]

Ashurbanipal's soldiers tortured their prisoners of war, sometimes skinning their victims alive. (Ashurbanipal also had these scenes devoted to art.)[3] This may have been part of the reason the prophet Jonah was so reluctant to go to Nineveh, the capital city Ashurbanipal made grand and powerful, and offer words of mercy to the vicious enemy.[4] In any case, Ashurbanipal marched across the world in the mid-seventh century BC, swallowing up land in Babylonia, Persia, Egypt, and Syria, swelling the Assyrian empire to its largest size.

In the book of Nahum—the one book of the Bible dedicated to denouncing Ashurbanipal and his atrocities—the prophet Nahum cries:

> Ah! City of bloodshed,
> utterly deceitful, full of booty—
> no end to the plunder!
> The crack of whip and rumble of wheel,
> galloping horse and bounding chariot!
> Horsemen charging,
> flashing sword and glittering spear,
> piles of dead,
> heaps of corpses,
> dead bodies without end—
> they stumble over the bodies![5]

Nahum predicts the defeat of Ashurbanipal's Nineveh and the collapse of Assyria, the shame of the proud empire.

But before Ashurbanipal fell, he dotted his expanding empire with monuments to himself. Their inscriptions lauded Ashurbanipal as the

---

1. "Assyria: Lion hunts (Room 10a)" and "The Dying Lion, a stone panel from the North Palace of Ashurbanipal." *British Museum*.
2. Franz, "Nahum and Nineveh."
3. Franz, "Nahum, Nineveh and Those Nasty Assyrians."
4. Jonah 4:2.
5. Nahum 3.

conqueror "who made the totality of all people speak one speech" and "made the unruly and ruthless kings speak one speech from the rising of the sun to its setting."[6] One speech: all the world speaking one language, thanks to the sword of Ashurbanipal. It wasn't enough to conquer the world, to occupy other lands; Ashurbanipal wanted the whole world speaking his language.

Now back to Genesis 11 and Babel. (Babel was presumably Babylon, the great empire that defeated the mighty Assyria.) The story begins, in the King James Version, "And the whole earth was of one language, and of one speech." Think of all the predecessors of Ashurbanipal, all the emperors in the ancient world, their military campaigns, their inscriptions promoting their claims, or at least aspirations, to make the whole world speak their language. And think of how the ancient Israelites, with these emperors always lurking at their borders (before finally crashing through and taking the Israelites to exile), listened to the story of Babel over and over, with its human ambition to establish "one speech."

With this historical background, "one speech" was less likely a description of a perfect world, and more likely an ominous imperial campaign the Israelites feared. "The one-speech motif [is] identified with oppressively imposed conformity," write David Smith and Barbara Carvill. "It is by no means clear that Genesis 11:1 reports the kind of golden age that many in the modern era have glimpsed in it."[7]

So to answer the key questions of this chapter: What would a whole world speaking the same language be evidence of? Most likely imperial conquest. Who would be the most happy with that? The conquerors. The Ashurbanipals of the world. Who would be least happy? Not only the conquered, who have been robbed of their native language, but ultimately God, who delights in diversity. Divine intervention is needed to break the imperial linguistic hold on the world. Old Testament scholar Walter Brueggemann says that

> the Babel campaign attempts to establish a cultural, human oneness without reference to the threats, promises or mandates of God. This is a self-made unity in which humanity has a "fortress mentality." It seeks to survive by its own resources. It seeks to construct a world free of the danger of the holy and immune from the terrors of God in history. It is a unity grounded in fear and

6. Smith and Carvill, *Gift of the Stranger*, 211.
7. Ibid.

characterised by coercion. A human unity without the vision of God's will is likely to be ordered in oppressive conformity. And it will finally be "in vain."[8]

The theme of imperial oppression and self-worship keeps appearing in the story of Babel. "Come, let us build ourselves a city, and a tower with its top in the heavens, and let us make a name for ourselves," the builders say in verse 3. The tower might be a Babylonian ziggurat (a temple), or just the ancient equivalent of a "skyscraper."[9] Either way, it strains credulity to think that the height of this structure makes God feel threatened, as many tellers of this story suggest. "The Lord *came down to see* the city and the tower, which humans had built," says verse 5. The problem is not the height of the ziggurat or skyscraper, which is apparently puny. The problem isn't the altitude; it's the ambition—the ambition to "make a name for ourselves"—the dream of every Ashurbanipal and Alexander the Great as they trample the world, spreading their "one speech." The problem is self-importance. The problem, as it was in Eden, is pride.

God's intervention at Babel, in this context, is not jealous intrusion but loving prevention. "So the Lord scattered them abroad from there over the face of all the earth, and they left off building the city." The empire is shattered, the arrogance is humbled, and most importantly, the oppression of conformity is lifted. The people again spread across the earth. And each speak their own language, not out of disorienting confusion but out of an abundance of God's good diversity.

"As the empire is dismantled, maybe it will be possible to build human community again," writes Smith.[10] He notes that the very language of the Babel story suggests creativity's triumph over conformity. "The linguistic virtuosity of the Hebrew narrative in Genesis 11, with its careful structure, and its puns, alliterations and plays on sounds, underscores the note of hope by its display of creativity." We will talk more about linguistic creativity in Hebrew, and what it suggests about Scripture and about God, in chapter 7. For now, let's trace the Babel story beyond Genesis, throughout the rest of the Bible.

---

8. Brueggemann, *Genesis*, 99.
9. Smith and Carvill, *Gift of the Stranger*, 212.
10. Smith, "What Hope After Babel?"

PENTECOST: BABEL CONTINUED

At Pentecost, will God's action be a continuation of or reversal of God's action at Babel? According to the traditional reading, it's a reversal: at Babel, God cursed a harmonious world with multiple languages, now God blesses the world with them. But if confusion of languages were the curse, then the blessing might well have been what Smith calls "a miracle whereby the hearers were enabled to understand a single speech, where linguistic uniformity was restored."[11] But something very different happens. Is God conceding to linguistic confusion, changing his mind about diversity, or something else?

With the reading of the Babel story described by Smith and Carvill, we can trace an unbroken line from Genesis 11 all the way to Acts 2 and beyond. God's mandate is that his creatures spread across the world and delight in diversity. That was God's will in Genesis 11. That was God's will in Acts 2.

Smith notes the parallels between the two stories. Specifically, in both stories, Smith points out, "we have people gathering together. In response, God comes down. Confusion is said to ensue, and the sequel is dispersion."[12] He also observes that in both stories, the multiplicity of languages is somewhat gratuitous—the people in Genesis 11 could have continued to function with an official imperial language; while at Pentecost, most hearers would have understood Aramaic or Greek, so there was not an insurmountable language barrier. And yet, Smith says, "the gift of tongues affirms the linguistic individuality of the hearers."

Smith concludes, "The least that we can learn from Pentecost is that our solutions to the fragmentation which we face will not be genuinely redemptive if they trample upon human diversity, including diversity of language." Linguistic diversity is not the threat to world unity that it is often made to be; linguistic conformity is not the key to world peace that it is often made out to be. As Smith observes:

> [Linguistic] dysfunction [is commonly] attributed to the speaker of the alien tongue, the "barbarian" who lacks full humanity. The embrace of all languages as meaningful [in Scripture] counters the common human tendency to define humanity in terms of the ability to speak the definer's language and the tendency in subsequent church history to regard most vernaculars as too uncouth

11. Ibid.
12. Ibid.

to carry God's truth. On more than a few occasions through history the church has behaved more like Assyrian rulers, imposing a single language on subject peoples and persecuting and imprisoning champions of the vernaculars, than like the Spirit-filled group of disciples on the day of Pentecost. Once again the warning dimension of the Babel narrative turned out to be needed.[13]

It is tempting, and perhaps natural, to assume that linguistic conformity—a world speaking the same language—would be a harmonious one. But given human nature, which is prone to division under sin, we could reasonably predict that linguistic unity would be undermined by new divisions (rifts according to accent, geography, social class, or something else). And given this new reading of Babel and Pentecost, we can see an even more troubling aspect of attempts at linguistic unity; they are often motivated by pride and power. God blesses us with linguistic diversity—intervening when necessary to ensure it—as a counteractive measure to imperial conformity.

REVELATION 7: THE END OF THE BABEL STORY

Revelation is how the Bible, and the story of God's plan for creation, comes to completion. Revelation is not just a prediction of events at the end of the world; it is a vision that wraps up the whole biblical story, a vision for a renewed creation, which is the vision that directs our worship and our work in the world.[14]

> After this I looked and there before me was a great multitude that no one could count, from every nation, tribe, people and language, standing before the throne and in front of the Lamb. They were wearing white robes and were holding palm branches in their hands. And they cried out in a loud voice: "Salvation belongs to our God, who sits on the throne, and to the Lamb."[15]

The throng of victorious believers, from every tribe and tongue, join in a common song, each in their own language, and sing the praise of God. This, the eternal harmony of linguistic diversity, is the destiny of God's people. This is the fulfillment of God's plan.

---

13. Ibid.
14. See Bierma, *Bringing Heaven Down to Earth*.
15. Rev 7:9–10.

This, finally is the closest the world will come to "one speech," as all voices join together. But they join in their own language, affirming their own individuality and identity. This is not linguistic conformity and monotony; instead, it is a choir of harmonious voices. Ashurbanipal thought the ultimate victory would be all the peoples of the earth praising him, "the king of the universe," in his own language. God thinks the ultimate victory is for people of every tribe and tongue to shout at once, in their own language. The true emperor sees conquest not in oppression but in the full flourishing of every human language.

Again, this story stands in direct succession after Babel and Pentecost. In both stories, God made a way for linguistic diversity. In both stories, the results of God's action was the multiplicity of languages on the earth. Now that plan comes full circle, and every language is raised in full voice to praise God. But this Pentecost flame will never go out; the multilingual chorus will keep shouting and singing, with no need for further intervention to make a way for diversity.

The call to the church is to actively hope for this day by beginning to sing this song already now. Again, Revelation is not just a distant vision, but a model for which the church must start striving. How can the church today sound more like the church in Revelation 7? What does it mean that the destiny of the church is portrayed as a multilingual chorus? What would a church that believed that look and sound like? The remaining chapters begin to explore this question, beginning with a call to linguistic hospitality.

3

Love Your Neighbor

The Ethics of Hospitality

Concern and love for one's neighbors is one of Christianity's defining characteristics. Unfortunately, this often requires a paradigm shift from contemporary culture's focus on individualism and selfishness. How we use language and our attitudes towards others' forms, functions, and use of their language should be shaped by our humble submission to the call of Scripture.

BIBLICAL HOSPITALITY

The place of "hospitality" is not usually thought of as especially meaningful in terms of the life of the church. If it is practiced at all it usually takes the form of inviting guests for coffee or dinner, making them feel welcome, engaging in good conversation, and perhaps hosting them for the night. The meaning of hospitality includes those ideas, but biblical hospitality can be seen as something more profound and significant than just offering a drink or a meal to someone, it was a way of life and vitally ingrained in the culture. One can find in Genesis many such stories showing the significance of hospitality. In Genesis 18, Abraham urges three visitors to stay with him. We find out that these visitors are actually God and two angels.

> The LORD appeared to Abraham near the great trees of Mamre while he was sitting at the entrance to his tent in the heat of the day. Abraham looked up and saw three men standing nearby. When he saw them, he hurried from the entrance of his tent to meet them and bowed low to the ground. He said, "If I have found favor in your eyes, my lord, do not pass your servant by. Let a little water be brought, and then you may all wash your feet and rest under this

> tree. Let me get you something to eat, so you can be refreshed and then go on your way—now that you have come to your servant." "Very well," they answered, "do as you say." So Abraham hurried into the tent to Sarah. "Quick," he said, "get three seahs of fine flour and knead it and bake some bread." Then he ran to the herd and selected a choice, tender calf and gave it to a servant, who hurried to prepare it. He then brought some curds and milk and the calf that had been prepared, and set these before them. While they ate, he stood near them under a tree.[1]

Abraham, Sarah, and the servants all act with urgency in their hospitality. In ancient times, guests didn't have to ask for food or shelter. Once a traveler made himself known, generous hospitality was expected.[2] The host would offer rest, refreshment, and a meal. In addition, it was assumed that the meal would be more than what was originally offered. There was also an implication that reciprocal hospitality would be shown if the roles were reversed.

The importance of hospitality in Old Testament society is also shown by Abraham's nephew, Lot, in Gen 19:1–8 when he urged two visitors (also angels) to stay with him, and by Job in Job 31:16–23 and 31–32 when he is telling his companions all of his good deeds. However, hospitality to others was not just practiced as a way of life during this time, it was also commanded by God. For example, the people of Israel are told by God in Lev 19:9–10 to leave some of the grain from their harvest and the grapes from their vineyards for the poor and foreigners. This is illustrated in Ruth 2 when Ruth, a foreigner from Moab, gleaned left-over grain for herself and her mother-in-law Naomi.

God's love and concern for the foreigner or stranger is profound. In Matt 25: 37–40, Jesus tells a parable about how men and women are judged. He says,

> Then the righteous will answer him, "Lord, when did we see you hungry and feed you, or thirsty and give you something to drink? When did we see you a stranger and invite you in, or needing clothes and clothe you? When did we see you sick or in prison and go to visit you?" The King will reply, "I tell you the truth, whatever you did for one of the least of these brothers of mine, you did for me."

1. Gen 18:1–8.
2. Walton and Matthews, *IVP Bible Background Commentary*, 44.

It is God's character to love and care for those in need, including the poor, widowed, and specifically foreigners. The Israelites were commanded to show hospitality to foreigners, because God loves them. God even commands the Israelites to welcome foreigners to worship with them in celebrating the Passover.

> An alien living among you who wants to celebrate the LORD's Passover must have all the males in his household circumcised; then he may take part like one born in the land. No uncircumcised male may eat of it. The same law applies to the native-born and to the alien living among you.[3]

Here we can see that God gladly receives worship from the Jew and Gentile alike. But God takes it a step further. He commands his people not only to welcome foreigners, but to love them radically, as they love themselves.

> When an alien lives with you in your land, do not mistreat him. The alien living with you must be treated as one of your native-born. Love him as yourself, for you were aliens in Egypt. I am the LORD your God.[4]

So, it is clear that hospitality is significant in the Old Testament and not surprisingly we see that it continues to be important to Christians in the New Testament.

In the New Testament the practice of hospitality took on a different look, especially after the church spread beyond Jerusalem. It went beyond a cultural norm to a hallmark of Christian virtue. Christians were urged to "practice hospitality" in Rom 12:13 and to "not forget to entertain strangers" in Heb 13:2.

It is easy to genuinely welcome those that are similar to you or that you find likeable. There are others, however, whom it is more difficult to welcome. Jesus gives the example of the Good Samaritan in Luke 10:25–37, who sacrificially cared for a severely beaten Jewish man after a priest and a Levite passed by and ignored him. Nowadays, the term "Good Samaritan" refers to someone who goes to the aid of someone in need. There are hospitals and nursing homes with "good Samaritan" in their names. In Jesus' day, Jews considered Samaritans half-breeds, despised and hated them, and commonly called them dogs. Yet Jesus

---

3. Exod 12:48–49.
4. Lev 19:33–34.

held up the example of the Good Samaritan as the one who loved his neighbor, demonstrating true Christian hospitality.

Who would be considered on par with the Samaritan example in our own society? In our day it may be argued that "illegal" or "undocumented" immigrants would fit a similar negative reaction. Christian scholars have attempted to give a biblical explanation to how the church should respond. James K. Hoffmeier attempts to make the case that the church can welcome the stranger into their midst, but argues that those who are in the country illegally must be encouraged to leave the country to follow a path toward being a "legal" immigrant.[5] M. Daniel Carroll R., on the other hand, argues that, especially in the case of Latin American immigrants, that it is more complex and that the U.S. immigration process is itself unjust in the way it handles the legal immigration process.[6]

We are not going to argue about immigration per se here, but we will offer an historical account of immigration to North America and the language policies relating to naturalization and bilingual education in chapter 4. Neither do we think that language is the only issue involved in the immigration debate. Obviously it is complex and multilayered dealing with aspects such as cultural, socioeconomic, and other areas of diversity. However, we are arguing that the language issue *is* significant. As we saw in chapter 1, language is at the core of how we bear the image of God and in how we form our identity. It is a powerful influence as we have seen in conflicts such as those in Catalan and Basque areas in Spain were as much *linguistic* struggles as they were political.

What we are saying is that since this issue is so much more profound than the "legal" versus "illegal" debate, we must address this from a linguistic angle. Our learning of languages and acceptance of languages should be despite this issue, not framed by it. We will, in our next section, explain the way we see the church responding to strangers and aliens in their community, through what we call *linguistic hospitality*.

LINGUISTIC HOSPITALITY

As we contemplate Jesus' command to love and welcome the foreigner, we see that the foreigner brought with him his "foreignness"—a different culture and a different language. Loving and welcoming the foreigner

---

5. Hoffmeier, *Immigration Crisis,* 158–60.
6. Carroll R., *Christians at the Border,* 131–34.

includes welcoming the foreigner's culture and language. In practicing linguistic hospitality, we are doing just that: making room for the languages of others, welcoming those languages, and acknowledging that language is a vital aspect of a speaker's identity. By the "languages of others" we refer not only to foreign languages, but also to distinct varieties within languages. Some examples of varieties of English would be Chicano English, spoken by some people of Latin American descent, African American Vernacular English, commonly known as Ebonics, and varieties of English spoken in different regions of the country, such as Appalachian English or the varieties of English spoken in the South. As stated by David Smith and Barbara Carvill, hospitality implies

> that the stranger not only will be greeted, but also will be given loving attention. The stranger not only will be fed and given drink; his or her voice also will be granted space. His discomfort will be met with concern, her stories will be heard and responded to . . . All of us have experienced the difference between homes where we are merely greeted with carefully measured civility and those in which we are genuinely welcomed, where there is authentic give and take. Maintaining a hospitable attitude means that we receive the representative of the target culture graciously and with love, and that we make space within ourselves for the stories and experiences he or she brings us from that culture.[7]

If you ask the average "person on the street," they would probably say that the world is becoming more diverse, tending more and more toward the "global village." If you look at demographic data in an increasing number of places in the U.S., many of the world's languages are represented there.[8] However, do our neighborhoods, workplaces, and more importantly, our churches, represent the diversity evident in our communities? Martin Luther King observed, ". . . I am ashamed to have to affirm that eleven o'clock on Sunday morning . . . is the most segregated hour of America, and the Sunday school is the most segregated school of the week."[9] Over fifty years later, we still tend to worship only with those of our own skin color, nationality, ethnicity, and mother tongue.[10]

---

7. Smith and Carvill, *Gift of the Stranger*, 91–92.
8. United States Census Data 2000.
9. King, *Testament of Hope*, 101.
10. Emerson and Smith, *Divided by Faith*.

Sociologist Michael Emerson studied[11] examples of multiracial churches[12] to see what factors were involved in their creation and sustainability. He argued that sustainability centered on the congregation embracing the vision for a multiethnic church and that mandated changes from external forces did not work well.[13] What was important was that the church's mission include the passion to diversify itself. It is interesting that neighborhood demographics were not the most important factor in predicting if a church could successfully diversify;[14] he states that

> [p]roximity is never enough, in and of itself, for congregations to racially diversify, but in combination with an impetus for change, such as the congregation's mission, it can lead to change.[15]

If a church wishes to become more racially diverse, it must be fully committed to doing so. Linguistic hospitality is a key factor in building bridges across racial and cultural lines to form lasting relationships. We have seen many examples of churches that have attempted to display some aspects of diversity, but for one reason or another failed in these attempts and reverted back toward a more homogenous congregation. For example, we have seen English language churches open their buildings to minority congregations. Sometimes the other services were planned for a time (such as a Saturday or late Sunday afternoon) in which no members of the English congregation were present. Other times there was a coordination of services so that while one congregation met in the sanctuary, the other met for a Bible study or Sunday school. In these situations there was very little, if any, attempt to fellowship among the congregations. It was painful to see, week after week, a silent passing of folk as one group left the sanctuary and the other group entered.

Sometimes we have seen some attempt to plan a fellowship between the congregations. This may be a combined worship service or meal. What we found was that if there was no attempt before or after

---

11. Emerson, *People of the Dream*.

12. Emerson defines a multiracial church as one in which any racial group does not comprise over 80 percent of the population.

13. Emerson, *People of the Dream*, 60.

14. Obviously there must be an available diverse population from which to draw people, but Emerson argues that a church can actually reflect more diversity than its neighborhood if its mission is appealing to those outside of its immediate area (55).

15. Emerson, *People of the Dream*, 54.

the services to build relationships, this also failed. In cases of meals, it was common to see folk from one congregation clustered around tables separate from those in the other congregation. Linguistic inhospitality was often a root problem in these situations.

However, we have witnessed some glimpses of successful fellowship among diverse congregations. One solution is for a church to embrace language teaching and learning for everyone. It isn't enough for a church to say that they will offer English as a Second Language (ESL) classes and expect that to be the whole solution. That is part of it, but the impetus for action should not all be on the foreigner or stranger. Linguistic hospitality would indicate a willing desire to learn the language of one's guest. So offering Spanish (or another language) as a Second Language would be a great first step. Churches who have embraced this example of language learning will avoid cases of "ships passing silently" as congregations pass and will engage in meaningful exchanges with people so that they will no longer be strangers, but friends.

In addition to language classes, it is important to see that the goal of a multiracial or multiethnic church isn't conformity. It isn't to integrate folk into a mono-racial, mono-linguistic, mono-worship-style congregation. The goal is a congregation that reflects God's diversity and creativity through its music, language, and culture.

CONCLUSION

Hospitality has been an identifying characteristic of Christianity from the start, with Paul's exhortation to "practice hospitality" and the Old Testament call to "welcome the stranger." Christians must combat segregation and injustice in society by practicing linguistic hospitality, rejecting monolingual isolation and welcoming those who speak other languages into their church and community.

4

From Every Nation

Immigration and Language

THE IMMIGRATION DEBATE IS not a recent phenomenon, but something that has at times raged or simmered over the course of American history. As we argued in chapter 3, this issue transcends merely political actions, but at its core demands a biblical response, that is, a call for linguistic hospitality.

We see that through world history we can see countries legislating and enforcing what languages will be used in their lands. The United States has been no different in enacting language policies over the course of its history. In this chapter we will look at these language policies at the national, state, and local level. We are particularly interested in how the church has reacted to these language policies, especially as it relates to immigration, such as laws specifying the primacy of English (so called "English-only" or "official English" laws) and also the requirement for English literacy for naturalization. Laws and policies relating to languages used in schools and specifically bilingual education will be covered in chapter 5.

We will analyze the role of the church in regards to language policies as they emerged over the three periods of immigration following American independence. The first period of immigration was from the 1820s to the 1870s, which brought approximately seven million immigrants to the U.S., mostly from Northern and Western Europe.[1] German and Irish immigrants each comprised a third of immigrants at that time.[2] At the inception of American history there was no national policy in terms of designating English as the official language. At the local level,

---

1. Daniels, *Coming to America*, 122.
2. Ibid., 140.

communities had the freedom to enact their own local language policies, or to enact none at all.

The next distinct era of American immigration was from the 1880s to the 1920s which witnessed a growing sense of American identity among the public, and with it a deeply held conviction that there would be one language spoken in the U.S., namely English. Southern and Eastern Europeans formed the majority of this group of over ten million immigrants.[3] The idea that to be an American was to speak English took hold during this time. Especially hard hit were the large German communities at the dawn of World War I, but all foreign languages were also deemed "un-American" by this time.

We are currently witnessing the third major era of immigration, which began in the 1960s. Immigration policy moved away from a strict quota system that discriminated against those peoples not already represented in the United States. With the removal of that system, the United States saw a surge of immigration from countries in the Eastern Hemisphere and from Latin America. The dropping of immigration quotas and large influxes of immigrants from all over the world have continued the tension between America as a place of welcome for all people and the struggle to keep a sense of an American identity. We still see today a struggle between this multi-cultural society and an American public's understanding of what it means to be American.

Throughout all of these periods, the church has been an integral part of American society. This chapter will discuss how the church has handled and reacted to these language policies. We will also analyze the current state of affairs and discuss how churches can respond biblically to our increasingly diverse world.

1820s TO 1870s: THE EMERGENCE OF POST-COLONIAL AMERICA

Historical Background

Historically, the first period of American immigration occurred during the Colonial period, where we find colonists primarily from the British Isles. However, there were pockets of German settlements in Pennsylvania and Dutch settlements in New York. Following the War of Independence and the War of 1812, the flow of immigration to the

---

3. Daniels, *Coming to America*, 188.

newly-formed republic regained momentum as immigrants sought a new life in the young republic.

The first major wave of European immigration to the newly formed United States of America started in 1816 with an influx of Irish immigrants. Between 1820 and 1900 an estimated 10 million immigrants entered the United States, over 4 million of whom were Irish.[4] Their main reasons for coming to the U.S. were the famine (and its devastation to the potato crop) and the difficulty finding land to cultivate in Ireland due to overpopulation.[5] They settled primarily on the East coast in major cities like New York and Boston. By the end of the eighteenth century, the Irish population in New York, Boston, Philadelphia, and Baltimore made up over twenty percent of these cities' populations.[6]

Other immigrants during this period also flocked to urban centers such as Philadelphia and New York City, which received the largest influx of immigrants, but others ventured westward, moving to places such as the rich farmland of the Mississippi Valley. The Homestead Act of 1862[7] opened the gates of the far reaches of the Western frontier, filling the gap between the Mississippi River and California. Early in the nineteenth century, the Chinese began immigrating to California in large numbers.

Throughout this period, groups of the same nationality often stayed together and formed relatively homogeneous communities, first in urban centers, like the Irish in Boston and the Italians in New York City, but eventually moving to rural areas as they were able to save money for travel and farmland. This period also saw the forced emigration of African men and women from a diverse array of languages and cultures in Africa to North America. These men and women were often placed into heterogeneous language groups by slave owners in order to prevent them from using their native languages to plot their escape. This brutal treatment to these men and women caused the eventual loss of their native languages. What emerged was an African American English which became deeply ingrained into their new American identity. The intonation, rhythm, and some words reflected their African heritage, but became a distinct feature of their new American identity. We will see that

---

4. Shannon, *American Irish*, 28.

5. Kenny, *American Irish: A History*, 46.

6. Shannon, *American Irish*, 28.

7. For more information on the Homestead Act of 1862, see Porterfield (2005).

by the late 20th century a struggle to preserve this dialect or variety of English ensued.

Another issue that must be addressed during this time period did not deal with immigrants' languages, but in fact, related to the original inhabitants of North America—the millions of Native Americans representing hundreds of unique languages. We also see how their identity and culture was shaped by the forced acquisition of English at the expense of their native languages. We will see how national policies toward Native Americans affected their use of their native languages.

Language Policy

On a national level, during the early and mid nineteenth century, there was not a policy of designating English as the official language of the federal government. In some places local level allowances were made for multilingual governance. After the Louisiana Purchase, the Louisiana Territory was allowed to govern in both French and English. In the same way, at the end of the Post-Colonial period, California was able to maintain Spanish language rights alongside English.[8]

During this era, one of the largest groups of immigrants was German. German communities had German language newspapers and church services, taught German in schools, and had stores which sold German goods and food items. At the beginning of this time period, there were no laws or policies at the national level that mandated the use of English. At the local level, however, languages other than English were used in official capacities for things such as local government, the media, schools, and church services.

As the number of immigrants increased, opposition toward immigration began to build. As previously stated, two-thirds of immigrants were Irish and German, the majority of whom were Roman Catholic.[9] This gave rise to opposition groups such as the Know-Nothing Party (also known as the American Party) of the 1850s,[10] which campaigned

---

8. The California state constitution in 1850 states that official documents would be provided in both Spanish and English. There has been much debate on the status of Spanish language rights following the Mexican-American War and whether the Treaty of Guadalupe Hidalgo promised language rights to former Mexican residents in the new American territory. See Bikales (1994) for more information on the debate.

9. Carroll, *Routledge Historical Atlas*, 90.

10. See Desmond, *Know-Nothing Party*, for a historical overview of the Know-Nothing Party.

on immigration restriction against immigrants from Catholic or other non-Protestant countries. This mood of resentment against immigration built up to the first immigration restriction law, passed by Congress in 1875, which barred convicts and prostitutes from entering the country.[11] By this time it was nearly a century of immigration to the United States before policies at the national level were formalized.

Language Use, Identity, and the Church

During this Post-Colonial era of immigration, communities made up of mostly homogeneous groups of immigrants were established and developed. While new immigrants continued to come to the U.S., second- and third- generation Americans maintained at least a passive bilingualism[12] within these isolated communities.[13] Strong identity toward the country of their heritage was maintained through language and customs. Ethnic food played a strong role in their cultural identity, as did ethnic stores, social clubs, and—most importantly for some—the church.

We can use the Norwegians as a case study of immigrants who exemplify this pattern during this time period. Since Norway borders the Atlantic, it was easier for Norwegians to travel to America than it was for the rest of Scandinavia at that time. The first Norwegians arrived to the U.S. in 1825; the floodgates opened in 1836. They first settled in North Central Illinois, and for the first sixty years, Illinois was their primary destination. In the decades following, Norwegians also immigrated to Minnesota and Wisconsin. By the end of the nineteenth century, the Norwegians pushed west past the Rocky Mountains into Montana, Idaho, Oregon, and Washington.

Norwegians called their countrymen who wanted to go to the U.S. the ones with "America fever."[14] Most Norwegian immigrants came to the U.S. for economic advantage, rather than because of poverty or political oppression.[15] Because Norway was an agrarian society at that time, economic prosperity was achieved through land ownership, widely available in the United States.

---

11. J. P. Smith and Edmonston, *New Americans*, 23.

12. "Passive Bilingualism" refers to the ability to understand spoken and written language, but a difficulty (or inability) to speak or write the language.

13. Haugen, *Norwegian Language in America*, 40.

14. Flom, *History of Norwegian Immigration*, 63.

15. Haugen, *Norwegian Language in America*, 18.

Throughout the nineteenth century, there were close-knit Norwegian communities comprised of mono-lingual, first generation Norwegian immigrants, along with their second and third generation children and grandchildren, who spoke both Norwegian and English. Typical communities had Norwegian language newspapers, church services, social clubs and schools. Community life was conducted in Norwegian. In order to function in the community and find one's identity in the community, one was compelled to speak Norwegian.[16]

The Norwegian Lutheran Church was founded in the United States in 1843. Throughout the nineteenth century, services were conducted exclusively in Norwegian. Einar Haugen, in his history of Norwegian immigration in the United States, writes of the importance of the Lutheran church in the Norwegian immigrant community. He stated that "the first and most persistent of the immigrants' institutions was the Lutheran Church . . ."[17] and that "the church provided an outlet for much of the social energy of the immigrants."[18] The use of Norwegian, especially in the Lutheran Church, remained largely unchanged during this first period of immigration. We will see that as America moved into the twentieth century, Norwegian identity was slowly being eclipsed by a growing sense of American identity.

AN EMERGING AMERICAN IDENTITY: THE 1880s TO THE 1920s

Historical Background

After decades of immigrants from primarily the British Isles and Northern Europe, an influx of immigrants began to come from Southern and Eastern Europe. In particular between 1890 and 1920 there were an estimated four million Italian immigrants to the United States.[19] Other groups that immigrated in large numbers during this time were from Greece, Poland, and Russia.[20]

---

16. Ibid., 42.
17. Ibid., 33.
18. Ibid., 34.
19. Daniels, *Coming to America*, 189.
20. Edmonston, *Statistics on U.S. Immigration*, 24.

Language Policy

More and more native-born Americans believed the swelling flood of immigrants threatened the nation's unity. Hostility which boiled over against the Chinese in the 1870s now turned against Jews, Catholics, Japanese, and finally, the new immigrants in general. In 1882, Congress passed the Chinese Exclusion Act,[21] which limited the number of Chinese immigrants to the U.S. At that time, Congress enacted further immigration restrictions, increasing the list of banned immigrants to include beggars, the insane, and unaccompanied minors.

The two prevailing language-related issues during this period were the importance of literacy and idea of the English language as the unifying element in our country. As Americans saw America as one of the preeminent civilizations at that time, they sought to identify what it meant to have an American identity, both on a national and individual level. Many concluded that the key to an American identity was being involved in the political process. In order to be informed about current issues, literacy was of paramount importance. As a result, Congress began including proposals for requiring a certain level of literacy in order to enter the country. For example, there was a proposal in 1907 that every immigrant entering the United States must pass a literacy test. This proposal was later dropped. Finally, in 1917 a law was passed stating that immigrants must be "physically capable of reading: English or some other language."[22]

As Americans thought about the vast diversity of people already living in the U.S., as well as those continuing to immigrate, they asked themselves what would unify them as a nation. The answer was found in language: in fact, that English should not only be *one* of the languages spoken in the U.S., but *the only* language spoken there. In 1914,[23] President Theodore Roosevelt said, "We have room for but one language in this country, and that is the English language, for we intend to see that the crucible turns our people out as Americans, of American nationality, and not as dwellers in a polyglot boarding house." [24]

---

21. J. P. Smith and Edmonston, *New Americans*, 23.

22. Edmonston, *Statistics on U.S. Immigration*, 25.

23. In 1912 Roosevelt formed the Progressive Party (also known as the "Bull Moose Party").

24. Roosevelt, *Works*, 554.

The idea of the importance of English as unifying agent was applied to the language polices set by the Bureau of Indian Affairs in the late nineteenth century. The policy was enacted by forcing native American children to attend boarding schools where an "English only" rule was strictly enforced.[25] An 1868 report from the Bureau stated that "... schools should be established which [Indian] children should be required to attend; their barbarous dialects should be blotted out and the English language substituted."[26] In the execution of this policy it was not the goal to preserve the first languages of these children, but to create new monolingual English speakers who would be alienated from their families and communities as a result.[27]

At the end of this period of immigration, the concerns, anxieties, and fears of Americans about their national identity reached a boiling point with the advent of World War I. Countries at war try to foster feelings of nationalism to gain support and to unify the country against the enemy. During the First World War, non-American customs and the use of languages other than English were viewed with great suspicion. For example, in 1918, Governor William Harding of Iowa made a proclamation forbidding the public use of languages other than English "in public or private schools, in public conversations, on trains, over the telephone, at all meetings, and in all religious services."[28] He stated that the use of other languages "is resulting in discord among our own patriotic people and is giving our enemies an opportunity to hinder the work of our government during these critical times."[29] There was a fear of appearing disloyal or unpatriotic if one did not use English. This could even be seen in communities that changed the foreign names of their towns and streets. For example, Berlin, Michigan changed its name to Marne and cities with German street names often changed them to patriotic-sounding names like "Liberty" or "Freedom."[30] Einar Haugen writes the

---

25. Fillmore, "What Happens When Languages Are Lost?" 436.

26. Atkins, *Annual Report of the Commissioner of Indian Affairs*, 1887 (1992).

27. Fillmore, "What Happens When Languages Are Lost?" 436.

28. Derr, "Babel Proclamation," 106.

29. Ibid., 101.

30. In Milwaukee, Wisconsin, part of "Bismarck Avenue" was changed to "American Ave" during WWI and then later changed to S. 15th Street. Milwaukee County Directories (1870 and 1929).

following in regards to the Norwegian-American community, but the quote exemplifies the feelings of many immigrant communities:

> Americanization hysteria induced by the war acted to hasten the natural urge of the American-born to abandon their special traditions. The restriction of immigration was the handwriting on the wall, which is strongly reflected in the literature and historical writing that fills [the period during the war]. Institutions like the church rapidly turned to English, while foreign language newspapers gradually lost their strength.[31]

Language Use, Identity, and the Church

While the church still formed an integral part of immigrant communities, a new tension between preserving the immigrants' native language and integrating into American society emerged. Immigrants' sense of identity began shifting from a local identity based on their native culture to a nationalized American identity. Going back to the previous example of Norwegian communities in the U.S., the exclusive use of the Norwegian language began to change at the turn of the twentieth century. Sermons delivered in English rose from zero in 1900 to 22 percent in 1915. In 1918, the denomination started an English association in order to promote the use of English in its churches. At that time, 73.1 percent of all services were conducted in Norwegian. Within ten years, all official church documents were changed from Norwegian to English. By 1935, the English association was dissolved because it was deemed unnecessary, and by 1948, 61.2 percent of services were still in Norwegian.[32] The church saw a gradual change in language use over the first half of the century, beginning with a few scattered services in English promoted by the English association founded in 1918. The trend continued with parallel services offered in both languages, with Norwegian eventually trailing off to only a few Norwegian services. Sometimes the change was more abrupt, such as with the arrival of a new pastor who either wouldn't or couldn't preach in Norwegian. This de-emphasis on Norwegian iden-

---

31. Haugen, *Norwegian Language in America*, 28.

32. President Theodore Roosevelt wrote a letter to the board of Luther College in which he advised the Norwegians "not to cling too long to the Norwegian language as the language of the church ... the result would be that the church would lose the young people ... as it happened in ... the Dutch Reformed [church]" (quoted in Haugen, *Norwegian Language in America*, 224).

tity led to the dropping of "Norwegian" from its denominational title. It is now known as the Evangelical Lutheran Church of America (ELCA). The latest statistics from the ELCA state that in 2008 there were 10,396 congregations in the United States.[33] Of those congregations only two still use Norwegian as their liturgical language.[34] This means that since 1900 the percentage of Norwegian language services dropped from 100 percent to less than .02 percent in ELCA churches.

The Italians are another representative group of immigrants during this era of immigration. Primarily, Italians tended to move to cities, and to stick together in communities. They went to industrial centers like New York and Boston. In many ways, they followed the patterns of the Irish in those places. Often, the Irish did not look too kindly on the Italians, so the Italians created their own churches and social clubs.

The primary reason Italians immigrated to the U.S. was economic. At the time, most Italian immigrants intended to go back to Italy. Instead, they found that they had more opportunities for a better life in the U.S., and they sent for their families. Sicilians were looked down upon as a group in their home country, so many immigrated to the U.S. because of discrimination in Italy.

When they arrived in the U.S., instead of expanding westward toward the Central U.S. like the Norwegians, they remained in the urban centers of the east and west coasts. Italians, often from the same villages, would stay together in communities. For example, immigrants from Valledolmo mostly stayed in Fredonia, New York. The church there, St. Anthony's Church, is named after the church in Valledolmo. In each center of immigration, Italian identity remained strong. There were a few key components in each of these communities. One is the establishment of mutual aid societies. By 1910 there were hundreds of such societies in the U.S. These societies provided aid and services, as well as a place to socialize, many of these in Italian because the immigrants did not know English. Most of these societies were small, poor, and limited to immigrants from the same city or region in Italy. There were some older and wealthier societies that supported some of the earlier immigrants, such as *Unione E Fratellanza*, *La Fraterna*, and *Legione Garibaldi*.

---

33. Evangelical Lutheran Church (www.elca.org).

34. Norwegian Lutheran Memorial Church in Chicago, IL (www.minnekirken.org) and The Norwegian Lutheran Memorial Church of Minneapolis, MN (www.mindekirken.org).

The first generation Italian immigrants were monolingual Italian speakers. They acquired English very slowly. In many cases the wives did not learn English at all, living isolated lives within the Italian communities. Every urban center where Italians settled had its own Italian language newspapers. By 1914 there were more than a dozen Italian language daily newspapers in New York City alone. The largest of these was *Il Progresso Italo-Americano*, with a circulation of over 80,000. Unlike Norwegian Lutheran Churches, which served the Norwegian community and helped preserve the Norwegian language and culture, Italian Catholic churches in the U.S. served as focal points to integrate Italians into American society. Silvano Tomasi argues that the church, through the creation of Italian national parishes, encouraged immigrants to develop a sense of Italian-American identity, absorbed them into the mainstream of American Catholicism, and enabled them to take their place in the larger American society.[35] In 1899, there were 14 Italian churches in New York City. By 1918, there were 70 Italian churches, 750,000 members of the Italian Catholic church, and 15 parochial schools with over 10,000 students. By 1920, in New York City, of the 800,000 Italian speakers, more than 90 percent were members of the Catholic Church.[36] At that time, all Italian Catholic church services were held in Latin (just as in other Catholic churches). The Italian language was used in such areas as socializing and pastoral care.

OPENING THE FLOOD GATES OF IMMIGRATION: IMMIGRATION REFORM FROM 1965 TO THE PRESENT

Historical Background

America has been the destination of immigrants throughout its history. However, with new legislation dropping quotas based on nationality and loosening restrictions following World War II, America's borders were opened to more people from nearly all corners of the globe. In this current period of immigration, the U.S. has seen fewer immigrants from Europe and Canada, but has seen a large increase in immigrants from Asia and the West Indies. Today the largest groups of immigrants to the U.S. hail from Mexico, the Philippines, Haiti, China, the Dominican Republic, India, and Vietnam.

---

35. Tomasi, *Piety and Power*, 98–102.
36. Nelli, "Italians," 547.

Language Policy

The 1960s saw a radical shift in the American sense of identity from unity as homogeneity to unity within a rich tapestry of cultural diversity. By the early 1980s, however, the economic recession caused a surge of resentment against immigrants. Insecurity fueled the perception that immigrants were taking jobs away from native-born Americans. A call for English as the official language became increasingly appealing.

The modern "English-only" movement, which began in 1983 with the establishment of the organization called U.S. English by S. I. Hayakawa, former Senator from California, was not a conservative or liberal issue, but appealed to a wide range of the electorate across party lines. Its ultimate goal was to establish English as the official language at the state and national levels. This issue appealed to liberals with the argument that the English language is what unifies Americans from diverse linguistic backgrounds. Conservative proponents of English-only felt that this legislation was necessary to encourage immigrants to learn English like immigrants in the past had. To date 31 states have designated English as an official language.[37] At the national level, there have been several attempts by Congress to designate English as the official language of the country. Currently, in the 112th Congress, a bill has been proposed called the English Language Unity Act of 2011. It states, "All citizens should be able to read and understand generally the English language text of the Declaration of Independence, the Constitution, the laws of the United States made in pursuance of the Constitution," and that "all naturalization ceremonies should be conducted in English."[38]

Language Use, Identity, and the Church

Previously, we used examples of Norwegian and Italian groups of immigrants to explore the role of the church in the lives of immigrants. The number of those churches, as well as other social organizations, that functioned in the native languages of the immigrants they served gradually declined over time until almost none do in the present. One of the reasons is a lower number of first generation immigrants from those nations. The Norwegian and Italian churches in the United States have lost

---

37. Note that Hawaii and Louisiana have designated Hawaiian and French respectively as official languages alongside English.

38. See full information on H.R. 997 at www.govtrack.us.

their identities as Norwegian and Italian churches, and have assimilated into American society.

In the same way, for this last period of immigration, we will look at the example of the Hispanics in the United States. Given their proximity to the U.S., immigrants from Mexico and Latin America have steadily come since the early nineteenth century. However, the recent loosening of restrictions in immigration law and policies for migrant workers has increased the flow and amount of immigration over that time. We will see that there are similarities and differences between the current Hispanic church in the U.S. and the Norwegian and Italian churches of the past.

One of the similarities we find is that the immigrants who are coming to the U.S. are mainly Christian. The difference is that where there was overwhelming homogeneity in the denomination of the immigrants of the past, Norwegians being Lutheran and Italians being Catholic, Hispanics can find representatives in a wide variety of Christian groups, including Catholics, Baptists, and Pentecostals.[39]

There seems to be an underlying assumption among native-born Americans today that the current generation of immigrants, especially those from Latin America, is somehow more resistant to learning English than their idealization of their own immigrant ancestors. However, as linguist Carmen Fought has shown, the second- and third-generations of Hispanic immigrants are shifting to mono-lingual English use as quickly as previous groups of immigrants did.[40] If we apply this pattern, and look at the current landscape of Hispanic churches, we can deduce that there will be a reduction of Spanish use in Hispanic churches until they assimilate into the English-speaking communities that surround them.

CONCLUSION

We have seen that the Norwegian, Italian, and Hispanic communities developed in similar ways. They had neighborhoods, grocery stores, newspapers, churches, and schools in which the immigrants' native language was spoken. A logical conclusion is that when communities are absorbing first generation immigrants, there is a higher need for first

---

39. Pew Hispanic Center (2007).
40. Fought, *Chicano English in Context*, 152.

language support and preservation. Very few first generation immigrants are bilingual. They need services and support in their native language. Even during second- and third-generation assimilation, if there continues to be an influx of new immigrants, those new arrivals will need first language support.

Currently there are many Spanish-speaking churches in the U.S. If Hispanic immigrants follow the pattern exhibited by the Norwegians and the Italians, those churches will die out or be assimilated into English-speaking churches as second- and third-generation immigrants become adults and come into leadership in their communities. However, is this pattern a good one? Should churches compel or even encourage the development of monolingual English congregations? Is our language the basis of our unity?

What have been the policies of local churches toward serving the immigrant community? They have fit into a role as part of the community. The Norwegian ELCA first served the immigrant community with native language services. English services came much later as second and third generations abandoned Norwegian in favor of English. Similar to them with a few differences are the Italians at the turn of the last century. The services themselves were in Latin, but the Italian language was used in the community. As for Italian identity, however, the church helped bring Italians into the "American" culture.

The Spanish speaking community today is similar in providing support to recent immigrants in their native language. This has been a trans-denominational work and not limited to the Catholic church. Even denominations that have not had historically high numbers of Latino members, such as Baptists, have started Spanish speaking ministries and services.

What have such churches had in common over time? This does not need to be limited to just the denominations listed here and can include the historical work of the Christian Reformed Church to have services in Dutch and Frisian and recently in Korean. The common aspect is that the church served the community. The common theme over time is that the church has had ministries and services in place to help recent immigrants. Recently, though, churches have differed from the past in that churches have been offering a wider range of services and help.

What has been the role of the church to integrate people into the "mainstream" of American society? What also has been the impact of local and national laws and policies related to the use and teaching of heritage languages? At the local level some schools were started in the native language. This was particularly prevalent in Catholic communities. English has not been designated as "official" at the national level, though since the 1980s it has at a state level. Also, Iowa's "Babel Proclamation" during World War I was the first, and only, attempt of a state to outlaw the speaking of a language other than English. Also at the national level there has been a proposed requirement of passing an English proficiency test in order to become a naturalized United States citizen.

God does not just care about our inner spirituality, but also about social justice, including public policy regarding language and languages. Christians must model healthy public discourse about language policies, and speak out against policies that reinforce prejudice and marginalization. Christian communities must be on guard against nationalistic sentiments that prevent wise public policy regarding languages. Drawing on linguistic research and experience, Christians can reject the myth that bilingual immigrants pose a threat to a country's dominant language, advocate or provide training in English for immigrants to North America, and help immigrants cherish and protect their own cultural heritage.

5

Teach Your Children Well

Language in Education

It is not unusual to find stories of hyper-competitive parents trying to enroll their children into exclusive preschools. When interviewed, these parents may say that they only want the best for their children, to give them an advantage. "You get what you pay for" is what one parent shared, and in most cases the curriculum at these preschools includes foreign languages.[1] This trend has now emerged in very exclusive (and very expensive[2]) preschools. One of the goals is to produce children who can speak a foreign language fluently, thus giving them an advantage, both in the academic realm and the job market.

What is a typical reaction to this child by other people? Perhaps there is amazement that the child can speak a second language at so young an age. Perhaps there is jealousy, since some wish they themselves could be bilingual or that their children could be. In this situation, it could be thought that the child is very intelligent and even has an advantage over other children by having learned a second language so young. What if the parents teaching their children another language are not from an English-speaking, upper middle class family, but instead are immigrants who do not have English as a first language? What if the child is learning English as their second language? Would the reaction be different? Instead of amazement or jealousy, would the reaction instead be concern that maintaining the first language would impede the acquisition of English? Or perhaps anger is either overtly or covertly

---

1. "The Most Expensive Preschools," *Forbes* (September 19, 2007). Online: www.forbes.com.

2. At the most exclusive preschools in New York City the cost for tuition has reached upwards of $30,000 a year according to the Forbes article.

expressed over the fact that "people should just learn to speak *our* language," meaning English. However, bilingualism among children is very common around the world, perhaps even a typical situation beyond the borders of monolingual English-speaking countries such as the United States and England.

This chapter will address why multilingualism should be encouraged in our churches, even among children. Not only should immigrant children and adults be encouraged to maintain their heritage language while learning English, but English-language speaking families should also have the goal to learn another language. We need to move beyond an anglo-centric view of the world and affirm to our children that multilingualism, not monolingualism, is in fact biblical.

LANGUAGE AND IDENTITY

Our identity is shaped by our use of language, such as which language or dialect we use. In fact, we can talk about "identities" since language and dialect use can be adapted to a specific situation. For example, even in monolingual speakers, we can see a continuum in which speakers can go from formal to informal use. One can use a formal version at work and a more informal version at home or with friends. No one speaks exactly the same all of the time. Those who are bilingual (or bidialectal) can also adjust and adapt their speech depending on the context and to whom they are speaking.

Current theory on second language acquisition considers the role of identity to be critical in the process of language acquisition. Linguists see the identity of language learners as malleable and changeable. Whenever one acquires a language, either his or her first language or subsequent ones, that person is engaged in a process of identity construction. This negotiation is a life-long process and occurs in adults as well as children.

This focus on identity construction, made popular by the work of linguist Bonny Norton[3], gives a framework to the language-learning process. Older theories of language learning were based on binary paradigms such as whether language learners were motivated or unmotivated, introverted or extroverted, and other such aspects. For Norton and other scholars interested in identity research, the language learning

---

3. See Norton, *Identity and Language Learning*.

process is an interplay of social, historical, and cultural contexts in which learning happens. How learners actually learn depends a lot on how they react to these sometimes very diverse and divergent contexts. The difference between these older theories and the newer identity-based models and is that the former, with its attention to topics such as motivation, was primarily psychological in essence, while newer models were concerned with what is more sociological in nature. Norton posits that a language learner can in fact be very motivated to learn a second language, but ultimately fail to do so because of a lack of what she calls "investment."[4] For example, a family may desire for their children to become bilingual and acquire Spanish as an advantage for them. They may hold that the child may excel academically and perhaps can be prepared for a better job. However, if the parents and children are not invested in joining the Spanish-speaking community, or have hesitation in fully immersing themselves in the language and culture, acquisition will ultimately fail. In other words, language learning is more than just grammar learning, it is a decision to join a community of speakers. Therefore, the learner's identity changes as this new language and culture becomes a part of him or her. For children and adults to fully acquire a language, one must be invested in a language and its community of speakers. It takes a sense of humility to join a group rather than demand others to join your group. It is to this practice that Christians are called.

TEACHING AND LEARNING CONTEXTS

Parents are the single most important piece to this puzzle when considering bilingualism in their children. The choice to encourage bilingualism in children often begins as early as birth. We will see that school is also a vital part to this process, but again it is often parental initiative to place their children in a school that provides such language learning opportunities.

One clarification must be made from a linguistic point of view. Linguists would argue that adults don't "teach" children language (either their native language or subsequent ones in childhood) any more than parents teach their children to walk. This relates to the old nature versus nurture debate. Prominent linguists such as Noam Chomsky[5]

---

4. Ibid., 10.
5. See, for example, Chomsky, *Aspects of the Theory of Syntax*.

argue that humans are born with a genetically imprinted structure for language (and we would add that it is further supported by the idea that humans are made in God's image). So, due to our nature we are wired for language. Nurture does play into the equation, but it does not play as much of a role as we think. Children don't need to be taught long lists of grammar rules in order to acquire their native language, and the same holds true when acquiring a second language, if exposed to it at an early age. The key aspect is exposing them to the sounds, words, and sentence structure of the language. The easiest way is to follow a model such as the "one parent, one language" model where children get exposed to a different language from each parent. Often, though, the language that is least dominant in the community is harder for a child to acquire. For example, if a mother speaks Japanese and a father speaks English in the United States, it will be harder for children to acquire Japanese than English since there is a higher influence from English in the community.

A strategy to combat this obstacle can also be used if the parents both speak only one language well. It is to supplement the exposure to the weaker language through other means such as language-specific DVDs or CDs. A more effective plan is engaging in interactive activities. This can be done by scheduling play dates with children (and adults) that speak the other language. Encouraging opportunities for the children to practice the language will result in actual acquisition and retention of the language.

Another key component to child language acquisition of a second language is to place them into a school that supports learning that second language. Even with a strong family commitment to learning a second language, it often takes the school environment to implement a firm language learning foundation in the child.

There are a few models used to teach children a foreign language in school. These programs have the objective of student proficiency in the second language, not just exposing them to some words or phrases. There are bilingual education programs, as was covered in chapter 4, that were established to aid immigrant children to learn English with the goal of integrating children into the mainstream English classroom as quickly as possible. However, there are other bilingual education programs designed to facilitate English speaking children to become bilingual speakers.

One program is called Two-Way or Dual Immersion. This type of program is designed to help both native and non-native English speakers to become bilingual and biliterate. In this case all students are in the same boat—spending half of their time learning another language. The native speakers of both languages help the others learning theirs. It puts both groups on equal footing. This is a great resource to help non-native English speakers to solidify their heritage language by both maintaining the spoken language, and also learning it academically and increasing their reading and writing proficiency. Too often immigrant children who are forced into mainstream English classes end up functionally losing their first language. This program helps them maintain and strengthen their native language and their second language. For native English speakers this helps them learn two languages as well. Ideally a dual immersion class would be split 50/50, but in reality it is not always so.

In full immersion classes, non-native speakers are taught exclusively in the second language, but with support and help. Their classes are with other learners, not with mainstream native speakers. For immigrant children this does help them learn a second language like English, but no support is offered for their first language. Native language loss is often the case. Two-way or dual programs are a much better option for heritage language maintenance. For speakers learning a second language in which they are immersed in a minority language, this can be quite effective. For example, native speakers of English in programs learning Spanish or Chinese can be effective in maintaining their English because of the support they get at home and in the community.

WHY YOUR CHILD SHOULD BE BILINGUAL

There have been several arguments put forth by those who either dismiss the need for bilingual children in the United States or who argue that, in fact, it is harmful to their development. The first argument commonly put forth either overtly or passively through inaction is that a knowledge of English is all a child needs to know if they grow up in America. There are a few thoughts on why this argument persists. First, as we covered in chapter 4, English has been viewed as a unifying element in a country made up of a melting pot of languages and cultures. Some have seen bilingualism as a step away from the unity that English provides. Another thought is that English is a global language, so that if everyone else is learning English, why would Americans need to take the time or effort to learn another language? However, while English is a popular language and an estimated 322 million people are speakers of English,[6] it is not true that all or even most of the world's population is functional in English.[7] In fact, more people in the world are multilingual than are monolingual.[8]

The second argument put forth against childhood bilingualism is that learning two languages at once will cause interference and harmful mixing with a child's first language. It is a fear based on the false premise that childhood bilingualism is somehow unnatural or unusual. However, children have been shown to be able to not only be successfully bilingual, but can also be fluent in three or more languages depending on the language community.[9] Also, it is completely natural for developmental mixing of languages to happen. Just as monolingual children make generalizations and educated guesses by saying *foots* for *feet* or *goed* for *went*, bilingual children may understand the English word *after* to mean "before" due to its similarity in structure to the Spanish word *antes*, "before."[10] A related argument is that parents should wait to introduce a second language to a child until their first language is established.

So what are the reasons parents should encourage bilingualism in their children? There are several arguments given. First, it is argued that second language learning be started in children since research has shown that starting earlier is better for ultimate proficiency.[11] There is an idea of a "critical period" in which there is a window of time (usually thought to be before puberty) in which it is ideal for children to acquire language.[12] Attempting to learn a language after that time is considered to be more difficult, with native-like proficiency being nearly impossible.[13] This is a crucial argument given for why bilingual education programs should be

---

6. SIL, *Ethnologue*, 14th ed., 2000.
7. Ibid.
8. Tucker, "Global Perspective on Bilingualism and Bilingual Education," 1.
9. Ibid, 2.
10. This example is taken from the author's (MP) children.
11. King and Fogle, "Raising Bilingual Children," 1.
12. The classic argument of the Critical Period Hypothesis can be found in Lenneberg, *Biological Foundations of Language* (1967).
13. See Bialystok and Hakuta, "Confounded Age," for an in-depth treatment on this topic.

offered for elementary aged children—it is the optimal time for language learning.

The second argument given for why parents should encourage children to be bilingual is that general cognitive benefits have been shown to result in bilingual children. Research has indicated that they have earned higher SAT scores,[14] have improved problem-solving skills,[15] and have increased creativity[16] when compared to monolingual peers. This is a reason why many exclusive preschools and elementary schools offer foreign language classes, in order to help give their students a well-rounded educational experience that will enable them to excel academically.

The third argument is that there can be an economic advantage in the long term for students. Bilingualism can be seen as a unique skill that can be put on a resume and can prepare one for the job market. Also this can include the ability to communicate with others while traveling or to greet guests who visit their community.

The fourth argument, for those from a non-English speaking background in particular, is that bilingualism can connect people with their cultural heritage. It can allow closer relationships with relatives who may not know English well, but can also cultivate a person's identity in relation to their heritage. They would not just be an "American," but a Japanese-American who can speak Japanese or an Italian-American, able to speak Italian.

Our view is that these benefits to learning a second language are all great things, especially in the deepening of ties to one's cultural heritage. However, we view these as by-products or bonuses, not as the primary motivation for bilingualism for Christians. When parents choose to help train their child to be a bilingual speaker, they are recognizing the process as something deeply spiritual. When a child is learning another language, they are engaged in discipline and study in a way that leads to maturity and wisdom. What happens when children are in the process of learning a new language? They are exposed to new words, ideas, and ultimately a new comprehensive culture of people who speak that language. We stated earlier that the language learning process itself was one of identity formation. This can go even deeper and be considered at a spiritual level. There is an ancient Jewish saying from the first century

14. The College Board SAT, 2003.
15. Bamford and Mizokawa, "Additive-Bilingual (Immersion) Education."
16. Ibid.

that "study is worship."[17] The act of learning and the discipline needed are themselves acts of worship. Also, as we will see in chapter 6, by entering into a new language and culture, we can join the universal church in that act by displaying a more diverse liturgy.

When our children learn languages they are opening themselves up to a world of ideas. One of the outcomes of bilingualism is not only an appreciation of diversity, but an expectation of diversity in the world. Research has suggested that bilingual children are more willing to accept multiple words for things[18] (i.e., they accept ambiguity better and are curious about how things are said in more than one way), whereas monolingual children hold more strictly to the idea that a thing can only be identified using one label. Ambiguity and having more than one word for something are difficult for these children to accept. Multilingual children expect diversity. There is an appreciation that leads to acceptance and expectation of wanting to learn more and more about God's great creation, more about words and ultimately the Word.

CONCLUSION

Parents and teachers must see that language use is one of the ways their children and students bear the image of God. Teachers must nourish their students' identity and implement strategies that support, rather than destroy, students' formation of self-identity through language use and culture. Christian teachers can draw on language pedagogy and teaching philosophy to learn how students' choice of language use is an act of forming or expressing their identity.

---

17. We owe the background to this quote to our colleague Scott Carroll, former Ancient Studies Professor at Cornerstone University.

18. Bialystok, "Metalinguistic Aspects of Bilingual Processing."

6

The Word of the Lord

The Language of Scripture and Worship

IN THE MAJOR EVANGELISTIC movie *Jesus*, often called "The Jesus Film," the actor portraying Jesus Christ—with well-combed hair and baby-smooth skin—speaks in impeccable British English.[1] His conversations, sermons, and monologues—even as his sandals get sandy, and his hearers are peasants—soar with the silky notes of a member of the British parliament.

The portrayal of Christ speaking English with a British accent may seem a natural choice for the moviemakers. British English, after all—at least the so-called "BBC accent," associated with British newscasters—sounds authoritative, noble, beautiful, and even holy to hearers around the world.[2] The idea of a religious figure, let alone a divine messianic one, speaking this way probably seemed fitting to many viewers.

The historical problems with this portrayal are clear. Most obviously, the English language didn't exist at the time of Christ. Jesus probably spoke mostly Aramaic, along with some Hebrew and Greek. Not only that, but being from Galilee, he spoke with a "northern accent," the accent that exposes Peter as a follower of his in Matthew 26:73. The northern accent was derided by southern Jerusalem dwellers as rural and uneducated, the same way the southern U.S. accent is in the United States. So Christ's status as wise religious teacher was probably undermined by the way he sounded, given the linguistic associations of the day. Having the Jesus in the Jesus Film speaking with a U.S. southern

---

1. Krish and Sykes, *Jesus*.

2. The distributors of the film did not, however, seek to promote English over other languages; the film has been translated into multiple languages in the course of its international distribution. Whether or not translators sought to use a more elite version of languages when translating into them is unknown but, arguably, likely.

twang would be more true to history, though it probably would have offended most viewers.

These details might seem like minor historical trivia, but they reveal a linguistic bias that continues to this day. Our tendency to see one language, and one accent of one language, as particularly authoritative, and even holy, remains mostly unexamined, even though it forms hidden prejudices. Whether these prejudices lead to outright discrimination and hatred or just subtle presumptions of superiority can be debated. What is clear is that to truly see every human language as God's gift, equally worthy of our attention and equally adequate for praising God as any other, we need to topple a sense of our own language or own accent being linguistically superior, even linguistically sacred. Just as we would never accept that one ethnicity is more sacred than another, more fit to praise God, or more preferred by God, we should reject the same claim for any particular language.

This chapter explores how these sacred associations, or misassociations, could be broken down, and what impact that could have on our linguistic outlook, and our Christian faith. We will look at the original languages in which the Bible was written—or spoken. We will raise some of the problems with available translations in English, and some of the inherent problems in relying exclusively on translations to read Scripture. We will end by imagining new ways of incorporating the original languages, and multiple contemporary languages, into our worship, to make our worship services more of an echo of Pentecost. As we do, we will be repeating the biblical move of battering the notion that only one people, one tongue, or one way of hearing God is proper, adequate, or sacred.

A QUICK TOUR OF THE BIBLICAL LANGUAGES

As chapter 1 mentioned, early rabbis imagined that the language Adam and Eve spoke in the Garden of Eden was Hebrew, and that Babel introduced alternatives to Hebrew. That's overly simplistic, though almost any attempt at a short history of language in the Old Testament must resort to some simplifications. For the sake of discussion here—and for the sake of simplicity in general church discussion—we will talk about Hebrew as the language of the Old Testament.

This generalization summarizes that fact that the people of Israel, from the time of Abraham (traditionally dated 1812–1637 BC) to the time of Nehemiah (who rebuilt Jerusalem in 445–444 BC), spoke in different dialects and accents, used different versions of the written alphabet, initiated and developed linguistic changes, and represented different points in the history and progression of what we think of as Hebrew. In fact, many historians presume that the Israelites adopted a new language, Aramaic, while in exile in Babylon, and that the vast majority didn't know Hebrew by the time they returned to Jerusalem. Some of the latest passages of the Old Testament, including portions of the books of Ezra and Daniel, were originally written in Aramaic.

So to say that Abraham, David, and Nehemiah all spoke Hebrew, in short, is like saying that King Aelfred (849–899 AD), Shakespeare, and Mark Twain all spoke English. They would be almost mutually unintelligible to each other, but yet they are connected by the common thread of a single language's sprawling history. And so we'll talk about Hebrew as a single entity, understanding the dazzling diversity that lies behind that generalization.

To get a feel for the sound of Hebrew, read this passage (maybe even try reading it aloud):

> *Bereshit bara Elohim et hashamayim ve-et ha-arets.*
> In the beginning God created heaven and earth.

Biblical Hebrew is known for its simple sound and structure, its ambiguity, its extensive use of the throat in producing sounds, as perhaps even this short passage illustrates.

Lois Tverberg highlights some core features of the language in *Listening to the Language of the Bible.*

- "Hebrew has a small vocabulary, and each word usually has a greater depth of meaning than the corresponding English word." She gives the example of the Hebrew word *bayit*, which is usually translated "house" but can mean "family," "lineage" (as in "house of David"), "place," "prison," "temple," and "within."

- "Hebrew lacks abstractions, so interesting physical images are used to express abstract ideas." She points to the description of the Israelites as "stiff-necked" rather than "stubborn." We saw this in chapter 2, where the story of Babel begins by saying, "The whole earth had one lip," presumably meaning "one language."

- "Hebrew often uses the same word to describe both a mental activity and its intended physical result." Hebrew uses the same word for "hear" and "obey," she points out, because often the result of hearing words should be to obey them.[3]

Already we can see the obstacles that face translators trying to translate this language in English, or any other language, especially another language from another language family, with different characteristics.

Another feature of biblical Hebrew is that it was almost always read aloud, not silently. In fact, the Hebrew word for "read," *qara*, means "call." This makes sense when you realize that very few ancient Israelites could read and write. And so, when we read, in Deuteronomy 17, Moses' command that Israel's future king read the scroll of the law, Moses says, "he is to read it all the days of his life so that he may learn to revere the LORD his God and follow carefully all the words of this law and these decrees." You could also translate that verse, "he is to *call* it all the days of his life," or at least, "he is to read it aloud all the days of his life." Commands like these are among the reasons for the emphasis on reading Scripture aloud that continues into modern Judaism.

This point is important for a few reasons. First, it is a reminder that Scripture was almost never encountered individually and privately in ancient Israel, but rather among a people, usually in worship or a public gathering. This can help remind us that we, too, best read Scripture in the company of a body of believers.

Second, and of more linguistic interest, this fact helps explain why Hebrew uses so much word play: in part it's because so much of the impact the language was meant to have was *aural*. As Gary Rendsburg says:

> [T]he biblical authors consistently opted for word play, especially the alliterative type, whenever the opportunity arose. When a choice of synonyms was available, the writers typically chose the word that produced the greater alliterative effect.[4]

Greek, on the other hand, is the language of logic, philosophy, and the original democratic political system in world history. And so the biblical Greek prose—especially the letters—tend to emphasize deliberative argument and precision of ideas. The biblical Greek writers generally use

---

3. Okkema and Tverberg, *Listening to the Language of the Bible*, 2004.
4. Rendsburg, "Wordplay in Biblical Hebrew," 137–62.

less ambiguity and wordplay than the writers of biblical Hebrew, though some biblical Greek is still inventive and alliterative. Paul's Greek prose, for instance, spans both systematic argumentation and doxological interludes (some of which may be quotes of early Greek hymns), and in a moment we'll look at the rhetorical beauty of a book likely by another author: the book of Hebrews.

To make a gross simplification, though, biblical Hebrew writers tended to see language as fundamentally an *art*, emphasizing imagination, while biblical Greek writers tended to see language as more of a *science*, emphasizing precision. Translations that try to make the words of both languages sound the same obscure this fact. (Granted, part of this difference is one of genre: the Hebrew Bible is full of poetry, the Greek New Testament has many letters. Still, even in common genres such as narratives and apocalyptic literature, Hebrew has a different feel.) So to best receive the words we read or hear from Scripture, we must appreciate the different rhetorical tools and strategies that typify the different testaments.

To get a feel for Greek, here's the first sentence of the gospel of John:

> *En arche en ho logos, kai ho logos en pros ton theon, kai theos en ho logos.*
> In the beginning was the word, and the word was with the God, and God was the word.

But again, although biblical Greek has a different feel than biblical Hebrew, this is not to say that Greek doesn't have a beauty of its own. The book of Hebrews, in particular, has long attracted the attention of commentators for its soaring rhetorical tone (we don't know the author, but one good guess is that it was Apollos[5]).

> Here's the opening verse of Hebrews in Greek:
> *Polymeros kai polytropos palai ho theos lalesas tois patrasin en tois prophetais.*

We'll look at the translation in a moment, but first, just note the sound of the words, especially the repeated use of the "P" sound. Thomas Long,

---

5. Ben Witherington makes a persuasive case for Apollos' authorship in *Letters and Homilies for Jewish Christians: A Socio-Rhetorical Commentary on Hebrews, James, and Jude*.

Bandy Professor of Preaching at the Candler School of Theology—and a powerful orator in his own right—picks up on this in his commentary:

> The book of Hebrews begins not just with a thought, but with a sound, the sound of a preacher's voice. When the first phrase of Hebrews is read aloud in the original Greek, we can hear with the ear what could easily be missed with the eye alone: the richness of its tones and the rise and fall of its melody . . . this has the unmistakable sound of a sermon. . . . Like the initial line of Lincoln's Gettysburg Address . . . these opening words of Hebrews display the cadence, the alliteration, and the keen awareness of the musical flow of beautifully spoken language that signal a carefully and poetically crafted oral event, a style that is sustained throughout the book. In black and white on the printed page, Hebrews appears to be a bit like an epistle, or even a theological monograph, but, when it sounds in the ear, we know immediately that we are not in the library reading an essay but in the pew listening to a sermon.[6]

The rhetorical feel of that opening line is nearly impossible to capture in translation. A word-for-word translation, clunky as it is, could be: "In many parts and in many ways in the past God spoke to the fathers through the prophets." Long captures some of the original alliteration in his own rendering of the opening line: "In many fashions and in many fragments in former times . . ." However, each of his alliterated words in that instance are archaic, and the sentence still has to start with a preposition, "in," that isn't alliterative, because of English syntax. The result is that every English hearer of this opening sentence—or any hearer in a language that can't capture this rhetorical feature of the original Greek—misses out on the rhetorical mastery of the preacher, both here and throughout the book of Hebrews. Now, to be very clear: this does not mean that modern hearers fail to hear the central message of the book, which is the sacrifice and priesthood of Jesus Christ. On a lesser but still significant level, it means that while most modern hearers can receive the *content* of the message, we miss on out the *linguistic features* of the way the God-inspired authors first spoke and wrote it. And given the emphasis we are placing in this book on linguistic expression as a way we bear the image of God, that is a significant loss. (In academic study, we should distinguish between *linguistic properties*—the words, syntax, phonology of a language—and *literary style*, or the artistic ways a

---

6. Long, *Hebrews*, 4.

language is put to use. However, the distinction can be blurry, and these two areas of study are usually combined in the fields of *rhetorical studies* and *discourse analysis*.) It's not just Hebrews that was meant to be heard aloud, and appreciated for its original sound. Every book of the New Testament, from the gospels to the letters to the prophetic book of Revelation, was meant to be read aloud, in a public gathering of believers. While more Greek Christians could probably read and write than ancient Israelites, still their main method of gaining access to Scripture was to hear it read aloud in worship.

And at least one of Paul's letters was actually meant to be held up and displayed in worship. In Gal 6:11, he makes a seemingly throwaway comment that has no connection to the verse before or after it: "See what large letters I make when I am writing in my own hand!"

Commentators generally agree that Paul had been dictating his letter up until this point, probably using a scribe (perhaps Timothy) who could write better than Paul could. But at this point, in verse 11, at the end of the letter, Paul seems to want to put a personal touch on the letter and writes this part himself. Either for emphasis or because he isn't as skilled a writer, he writes large letters.[7] The reader who is asked to read this letter to the Galatians is prompted to stop at this verse, hold up the scroll, and display it to the gathered listeners to show that Paul put his personal stamp on this portion of what they are hearing.

So much of this linguistic and rhetorical context gets lost in translation. The solution is not for every Scripture reader to become a scholar of the original languages, or for everyone to always use a massive study Bible with innumerable footnotes to explicate the linguistic context verse by verse (although such study aids are wonderful ways to help Scripture come alive). No, God has seen fit to have his proclamation be translated into every language of the world, and the core of the gospel message comes through loud and clear to all hearers, no matter what.

Instead, the purposes of identifying all these features of linguistic and rhetorical context are, first, to remind us that the original language and culture in which these words were first spoken contain numerous riches, nuances, and particularities that make the words of Scripture even more meaningful than we might imagine; and second, to remind us that any translation into any other language, regardless of its style, denominational affiliation, and other factors we use to weigh translations,

---

7. Witherington, *Grace in Galatia*, 439–43.

is imperfect at rendering the full linguistic character of Scripture. As a result, we cannot cling to notions of one translation being "more holy" or "more pure" than another.

Finally, the emphasis in ancient Israel and in the early church on the public reading aloud of Scripture, and the sound of the words, reminds us of the historical heritage and the theological importance of reading Scripture aloud in public. Historically, our ancestors' emphasis on public reading was in part due to limited literacy and publishing technologies. But beyond that, ancient believers knew that a God who spoke to them from a cloud at Sinai, and later, through an incarnate Son, a human being with a mouth and vocal cords, so valued the sound of language and the effect of hearing it with one's ears and not just scanning it with one's eyes, that something of God's own voice was animating the spoken word itself, achieving a special intimacy that silent reading cannot fully recapture. Since much of the Western church today practices silent individual reading of Scripture, this cultural gap must be noted, and narrowed.

Given these particularities of the original languages, how useful and reliable are the Scripture translations we use? The short answer is: useful and reliable enough for the gospel to be preached. The longer answer is that we need a discerning look at how we use Bible translations.

THE WORDS OF THE WORD

There's an old urban legend, first recorded in the late nineteenth century, about people who assume that Jesus and the apostle Paul spoke English. As the story goes, one Bible translator was asking a congregation for funds for a new Bible translation, when a farmer in the congregation retorted, "What's the matter with the good old King James version? That was good enough for St. Paul, and it's good enough for me." A later version of the story has Miriam "Ma" Ferguson, governor of Texas in the 1920s, speaking out on English-only legislation and saying, "If the King's English was good enough for Jesus Christ, it's good enough for the children of Texas!"[8]

Both stories may be urban legends, concocted to exaggerate the ignorance and nationalism of English-only proponents. But even if no one really believes that Jesus or Paul actually spoke English (which, of course, didn't exist when they spoke and wrote), it can be tempting, after

---

8. Zimmer, "Ma Ferguson, the Apocryphal Know-nothing."

years of reading, to hear a Bible translation in one's native tongue as most authoritative, most appropriate for Scripture, and even to think of it as the most clear or reliable version of Scripture available. With the decline of the teaching of biblical languages in some seminaries, and the ineffective and overly technical teaching of them in many others, pastors are often content to preach from a translation of the Bible in their own language, missing many particularities of the original text. And most other readers seldom stop to think about the distance—historical and linguistic—between the version of the Bible they're reading and the original.

Because of this blind spot, and because of the above observations about the original languages, it's worth remembering that translations are limited in how well they can reflect the original text of Scripture.[9] As we do, it's important to emphasize that any translation of the Bible done by skilled and knowledgeable translators is, at the very least, adequate for conveying the basic message of the Bible: God's graceful and redemptive intervention in a world torn apart by sin. It is rare that a translation issue will lead someone to a misunderstanding or misreading that would imperil their faith as a whole. Besides, the basic message of Babel, Pentecost, and the New Jerusalem, as we looked at in chapter 2, is that God's Word should and must go out to all people in all their own languages. The biblical story works against any notion that we should *only* read Scripture in its original languages. The Spirit speaks through the words of the Word, no matter in what language.

The central argument here is that translations nonetheless give us a linguistically limited rendering of the original text of Scripture, one that often obscures some of the rhetorical richness of God's revelation in Scripture. Translation does not interfere with the core gospel message being proclaimed, but it sometimes hinders subtleties, overtones, resonances, artistry, and emphasis in the original text, and as we saw above, that can limit the full rhetorical impact of Scripture. The Italian saying "traduttore, traditore" means "translator [is] traitor." It sounds extreme, but it's partially true: in translation, something will be betrayed. Not the core message, but some of the linguistic essence of the original.

---

9. Nathan reflects on this and reviews two approaches to biblical translation in Bierma, *Bringing Heaven down to Earth*, and "The Words of the Word." A more recent and comprehensive analysis is available in Fee and Strauss, *How to Choose a Translation for All Its Worth: A Guide to Understanding and Using Bible Versions*.

At times, the division between the message and the means used to convey the message gets harder to see. Samuel Meier argues that the Old Testament prophets' use of poetry to deliver divine prophecy is essential to understanding and receiving the prophecy properly.

> [P]oetry is generally recognized cross-culturally as a more formal register of human speech—indeed, a human universal—a more sophisticated mode of verbalization that requires special skills in its production. As such, it becomes a more appropriate medium for mediating divine communications that by definition transcend ordinary human patterns. The medium is very much the message, and can even become one criterion by which one can discern a supernatural origin. The medium in which Hebrew prophetic texts are written is central to the message they convey. Poetry in many ways is not even optional for prophetic texts, for in poetic texts, the sounds of words take on a heightened significance. Phonetic images contribute to all aspects of the prophetic message.[10]

What follows are some examples where something—usually minor, but worth noting—gets lost in translation to English. None of them are cause to abandon translations into English or any other language, but all of them remind us of the linguistic distance that lies between us and the original words of Scripture.

trample my sins

In Psalm 51, the repentant psalmist cries, "Wash away all my iniquity and cleanse me from my sin" (verse 2), and later, "Cleanse me with hyssop, and I will be clean; wash me, and I will be whiter than snow" (verse 7).

Linguist Suzanne McCarthy notes that the Hebrew verb for "wash" here is *kabac*, which means the washing of clothes. The word actually means "to tread, to trample underfoot," since that's how clothes were washed in ancient Israel. You'd put a dirty garment underwater and trample it to try to get it clean.[11]

That understanding of the original Hebrew word gives new appreciation and new force to the poetic imagery of this psalm. The psalmist doesn't just ask for a cleansing or a rinsing, but is saying to God, "trample my sins out, just like I try to tread on my clothes to get the stains out,

---

10. Meier, *Themes and Transformations*, 86.
11. McCarthy, "hyssop."

pounding and grinding them with my feet." (Given that this Psalm is attributed to David after his affair with Bathsheba and murder of her husband, a thorough trampling and not just a casual rinsing was indeed in order.)

The rendering of this psalm by the contemporary poet Calvin Seerveld captures this image:

> Scrub me utterly clean of my guilty wickedness!
> Make me pure from my wasteful sin![12]

The usually gritty translator Robert Alter gets at a similar idea here, but less directly:

> Thoroughly wash my transgressions away
> and cleanse me from my offense![13]

Most English translations, though, go with "wash me," which is apt but doesn't fully capture the impact and power of the original poetic image.

nephesh

As Lois Tverberg stated above, biblical Hebrew generally lacks abstractions and puts things in the most concrete terms possible. The ancient Israelite worldview also held that a person was a unified being, in which the spiritual and physical essence of a person were so closely intertwined as to be inseparable. The general Greek worldview, on the other hand, held that a human was a soul trapped inside a physical body, and that the soul longed to be liberated from its physical container. Most Western cultures have adopted this Greek dualism, which goes against the Hebrew idea of a human as a unified being.

When we get to the Psalms, then, and come across the English word "soul," we need to pause for a linguistic and cultural adjustment. Hebrew didn't really have a word for "soul" or "spirit," and certainly didn't think of a soul the way the Greeks would later, or many Western readers would today, as a separate spiritual essence contained in a physical container. So what's really going on?

In most cases, the Hebrew word is *nephesh*, which means self, being, or essence of a person. In fact, one way to translate *nephesh* is "neck," since the neck unites the head and heart, and is one of the most vital

---

12. Seerveld, *Voicing God's Psalms*, 56.
13. Alter, *Book of Psalms*, 180.

lifelines in the human body. Picking up on this, and taking note of the Hebrew preference for concreteness over abstraction, the poet Robert Alter at times translates *nephesh* as "throat." In Psalm 63:2, "throat" is probably the best possible translation:

> God, my God, for You I search.
> My *throat* thirsts for You,
> my flesh yearns for You
> in a land waste and parched, with no water.

Most English translations say "My soul thirsts." But technically a spiritual entity can't have a physical longing—unless you want to make "thirsts" purely a metaphor for inner longing—and again, the psalmist doesn't have much sense of an inner spiritual component that has longings separate from his physical desires. David is in the wilderness in this psalm, he's low on water, and he's not in the mood for spiritual abstractions. His longing for God is every bit as real and physical as his parched throat's thirst for water. Ours should be too. As Alter says:

> The King James Version, and most modern translations in its footsteps, has the "soul" thirsting for God, but this is almost certainly a mistake. The Hebrew nefesh means "life breath" and, by extension, "life" or "essential being." But by metonymy, it is also a term for the throat (the passage through which the breath travels) or, sometimes, for the neck. As the subject of the verb "thirst" and with the interlinear parallelism with "flesh," nefesh here surely has its physical meaning of "throat." The very physicality, of course, makes the metaphor of thirsting all the more powerful.[14]

Here is a case where the core of the message—God sustains us, his creatures—comes through in any translation, but the rhetoric and cultural assumptions about how that happens gets lost in translation. We need linguists and linguistics to help us recover, appreciate, and be nourished by them.

Logos

We saw earlier that the gospel of John begins by saying, "In the beginning was the *Logos*," which English translations usually render as "In the beginning was the Word." The full meaning of *logos*, is hard to capture in translation, in part because the word is so elastic, being used in so

---

14. Ibid., xxvii–xxviii.

many ways in Greek. ("Word" is itself elastic and versatile in English—it has different meanings in "spell this word," "any word from them?" and "open the Word," for example, but *logos* is even more so.) Here is how one lexicon traces the meanings of *logos* as it is used in the Greek New Testament:

> *logos*
> 1) of speech
>   a) a word, uttered by a living voice, embodies a conception or idea
>   b) what someone has said
>   1) a word
>   2) the sayings of God
>   3) decree, mandate or order
>   4) of the moral precepts given by God
>   5) Old Testament prophecy given by the prophets
>   6) what is declared, a thought, declaration, aphorism, a weighty saying, a dictum, a maxim
>   c) discourse
>   1) the act of speaking, speech
>   2) the faculty of speech, skill and practice in speaking
>   3) a kind or style of speaking
>   4) a continuous speaking discourse—instruction
>   d) doctrine, teaching
>   e) anything reported in speech; a narration, narrative
>   f) matter under discussion, thing spoken of, affair, a matter in dispute, case, suit at law
>   g) the thing spoken of or talked about; event, deed
> 2) its use as respect to the MIND alone
>   a) reason, the mental faculty of thinking, meditating, reasoning, calculating
>   b) account, i.e. regard, consideration
>   c) account, i.e. reckoning, score
>   d) account, i.e. answer or explanation in reference to judgment
>   e) relation, i.e. with whom as judge we stand in relation
>   1) reason would
>   f) reason, cause, ground [15]

This lexicon then adds a special note on the use of *logos* in John 1:1:

> 3) In John, denotes the essential Word of God, Jesus Christ, the personal wisdom and power in union with God, his minister in creation and government of the universe, the cause of all the world's life both physical and ethical, which for the procurement of man's salvation

---

15. Blue Letter Bible, "Dictionary and Word Search for *logos (Strong's 3056)*."

put on human nature in the person of Jesus the Messiah, the second person in the Godhead, and shone forth conspicuously from His words and deeds.

The lexicon adds this note: "A Greek philosopher named Heraclitus first used the term Logos around 600 BC to designate the divine reason or plan which coordinates a changing universe."

In Greek, *logos* was a word used in multiple ordinary ways to refer to conversations and decisions, and in the most metaphysical ways, meaning mysterious organizing force behind the entire universe. The translator's unenviable task is to pick a single word or phrase that captures this meaning. "Word" is a start, but only a start. Again, we need linguists and linguistics to unpack the full meaning of Scripture.

We can see how looking beneath the layer of our available or agreed upon translation of the Bible will uncover more insights, riches, and registers of meaning in the original words. We can also see that our existing translations don't exactly mislead us, but they also—necessarily, inevitably—under-serve us. This reality should dislodge any sense that our favorite biblical translation—or our language as a whole—is the most authoritative window into Scripture. Any and all translations are incomplete and imprecise.

WORDS IN WORSHIP

So how can we apply this linguistic knowledge in worship? How can we better hear the strums and rhythms of the words of Scripture? How can we acknowledge in public worship that our translations of the words of Scripture are merely that—translations?

First, we need to recover the original biblical languages in worship to whatever extent possible, and let them take their place as the only languages that have any prior claim (though again, not an exclusive one) on being the most direct vehicle of God's inspired Word. (That is, the biblical languages were the first and most direct means of God conveying Scripture to humanity; and yet, after Pentecost, other languages are blessed to be adequate to convey the gospel message.) This means regularly incorporating references and explanations about the biblical languages in sermons as they illuminate the meaning of the text. But it could also mean reintroducing a common shared vocabulary of untranslatable words, such as *nephesh* and *logos*. What if words like those, and maybe a dozen more, were taught and used as part of a church's working vocabulary, as a constant reminder of the linguistic heritage and distance between original Scripture and our translations of it?

Second, we need to recover the orality of Scripture, especially in worship. Reading the Bible silently, reading along while someone else reads it, or reading Scripture in an overly mechanical or somber tone all sap some of the rhetorical force and artistry of the original text. What if a church focused on oral proclamation of the Word, instructing hearers to listen rather than open their Bible while the Word was read, or encouraging more expressive recitations of Scripture in worship rather than dry readings? What if, in short, we restored the power of the word "hear" when we say, "hear the word of the Lord"?

Finally, we need to bring a variety of languages into the mix in worship to remind us that no one language can fully capture the full scope of God's revelation through his Word. We need to regularly incorporate multiple voices speaking multiple languages in the reading of Scripture. Pastors can consult other languages when studying a passage. A member can read a passage of Scripture in a different language than the congregation is used to hearing.[16] Even for churches who do not experience spontaneous speaking in tongues in their worship, using words from different languages (with explanation when necessary, to avoid incomprehension), is a way of honoring linguistic diversity. The more that different tongues are put into practice to praise God, the more worship resonates with the full picture of Scripture as encompassing every tribe and every tongue.

---

16. See more ideas in "Something Borrowed: Worshiping with the Global Church," in Rienstra and Rienstra, *Worship Words: Discipling Language for Faithful Ministry.*

7

Language Purity and Language Play

Beauty in Variety

In 1754, Philip Stanhope, the Earl of Chesterfield, made a dire declaration: "It must be owned that our language is at present in a state of anarchy."[1] He was talking about the English language, at the height of the British Empire, years before the United States would emerge to exert enormous (and many would say, poisonous) influence on English.

Concern about the quality, purity, or "state" of a language is present in most major languages, but it has always seemed most troubling to speakers of English. The biggest reason is probably that English has always been a mixture, a mongrel, of other languages and language families, and different nations and languages have always worried whether their influence was losing ground.

The problem is that what lurks behind a campaign for the "purity" of a language is often prejudice—the same kinds of prejudice we have looked at throughout this book. This prejudice is often more subtle and less malicious, and has the advantage of the support of powerful institutions, most notably schools and teachers. In fact, the campaign for the purity of English, in the form of teaching Standard English in composition classrooms as a morally superior form of English, arguably represents the last acceptable prejudice in North American society.

In looking at the battle of standardization versus variation in North American English, we must be clear not to demonize Standard English the way Standard English proponents often demonize non-standard English. We must also continually affirm that teaching Standard English, in the right context, is not only appropriate but healthy for society.

---

1. Crystal, *Fight for English*, 74.

Proficiency in Standard English is indeed a worthy and necessary educational goal.

The problem is when Standard English is held up as a moral measurement, and when non-compliance with Standard English is seen as a moral failing. When instruction in Standard English is framed as the teaching of "the right way" to speak and write, when the emphasis is placed on avoiding "errors," and when a lack of, or waning, compliance with Standard English is seen as signifying "the decline" of the English language—when this is the context for teaching Standard English—then the effort is barely distinguishable, linguistically and ethically, from English-only campaigns and other forms of language prejudice we have explored. The result, again, is to exult in monotony and disparage diversity.

The fallacy in exaggerating the importance of Standard English is fundamental: language cannot be rigidly programmed like a machine. People vary, the words and styles and sounds of their speech vary; a language is as diverse as the people who use it. The attempt to enforce conformity hints at what we saw in chapter 2, when King Ashurbanipal of Assyria tried to enforce "one speech" on the people in an imperial campaign for linguistic monotony. But the opposite of an imperial attempt to enforce monotony is to delight, as God does, in all the beautiful ways that creative linguistic expressions add to the beauty of God's creation.

Conflict between standard versus non-standard dialects of English is of central interest to sociolinguistics, or the study of language in society. Sociolinguists study social factors behind language variation and change, including social attitudes toward language variation and change. Just as a sociolinguist wants to know how a society discusses and decides issues such as declaring an official national language, and the social attitudes towards different languages, a sociolinguist wants to know how a society discusses and decides which dialect of a language will be privileged, and the social attitudes towards different dialects. This is not to suggest that dialect differences are as important as language differences, much less that dialects are languages. It is instead to observe that sociolinguists have much to tell us about social patterns that affect language use, especially language variation, and that Christians can learn from sociolinguistic study in seeking to affirm linguistic diversity.

Considering Standard English to be a dialect may seem strange. We often think of dialects as deviations from the norm, with Standard English as the norm. We may also think of dialects as organic and devoid of strict rules, while Standard English is taught in a classroom and is supposed to follow strict rules.

The sociolinguistic reality, however, is that Standard English is a shared, socialized, specialized way of using the language, defined by distinctive patterns and features—just as any dialect is. And despite claims that it is superior or "more correct," there is no sociolinguistic reason why Standard English should be the preferred or "best" dialect of North American society (and now, by extension, the world), except that it is the preferred dialect of business, government, education, and other institutions of power. The "correctness" myth—the myth that Standard English is the "correct" way to use English—serves the interests of power but obscures the beauty of diversity.

No sociolinguist would deny that Standard English is considered to be the norm in North American society, and that using Standard English well in the environments and social groups that expect it is fundamental to thriving in North American society[2]. No sociolinguist would suggest that teachers should neglect to emphasize the social usefulness of Standard English. What a sociolinguist would reject is the claim that Standard English is inherently better than other English dialects, that its use is a good measure of a society's health, and that variation from this norm is a threat. All of these claims, however, are widespread, and have been throughout the history of English.

In addition to the sociolinguistic reality of dialect diversity within a language—and our biblical appreciation of diversity—Christians are called to linguistic hospitality, as we explored in chapter 3. Such hospitality need not include considering errors in Standard English to be legitimate alternatives to normal usage of the dialect, nor even necessarily the use of other dialects in settings where Standard English is expected. What linguistic hospitality should involve is a tolerance of, interest in, and celebration of other dialects as legitimate linguistic expression, and as part of a larger tapestry of a language. It would be incoherent to claim to practice hospitality while rejecting any use of non-standard dialects.

---

2. However Sri Lankan Sociolinguist Suresh Canagarajah in his book *Resisting Linguistic Imperialism* (e.g., 3, 86, 126) does challenge the notion of basing a "standard" English in a third-world context on a North American or British variety.

"Making room" for others means making room for the varied ways others communicate, and asking others to make room for our varieties of expression as well.

While the longing for purity in English is as old as English itself, the campaign to begin enforcing common norms through education gained power in the 1700s. Tellingly, this coincided with an explosion in population and urbanization in late medieval England, which produced (or exposed) a variety of new accents, dialects. It also coincided with the rise of the printing press and mass literacy, which ceded some of the power of writing to the masses, challenging previous patterns of linguistic authority. Philip Stanhope, the Earl of Chesterfield, quoted above as denouncing "a state of anarchy" in English, was one of the most passionate voices for the need for enforceable language norms. He insisted that an authoritative figure and authoritative text be established for the English language. As he put it: "The time for discrimination seems to be now come. Toleration, adoption, and naturalization have run their lengths. Good order and authority are now necessary.[3]"

Stanhope's solution was that the pioneering dictionary-maker Samuel Johnson be granted a "dictatorship" to establish common norms and rules for using English, and vowed, "I will implicitly believe in him as my pope, and hold him to be infallible while in the chair."[4] Johnson was not exactly christened in such a way, but many seized on Johnson's model of doing dictionaries as a way to establish linguistic order. Compositional manuals also became more prominent in schools, listing grammatical rules that supposedly produced good English.

The reasons for pursuing standardization in language then, in the 18th Century, and now, are partly the panicked reactions of those in power and those bearing prejudice toward lower class speakers. But in part, they are understandable and defensible social initiatives. Providing a common means of mutually comprehensible communication is a natural and important priority, especially in a quickly growing and diversifying nation, as England was in the 18th century and the United States is now. The Babel question remained: don't we need a common speech?

The answer, then and now, is a partial yes. Yes, we need a common means of communication for mutual comprehension, for basic social functions and purposes (like business, education, and government).

3. Ibid., 83.
4. Ibid., 86.

But we do not need "one speech" at the expense of diversity and variety. We do not need to dilute a multi-colored linguistic world with a single shade of gray. The attempt to enforce standardization in the teaching of English composition—and especially, to promote it as pure and morally superior—sadly promotes this shade of gray at the expense of beauty.[5]

And yet the contemporary movement for the purity of English and the superiority of Standard English persists, motivated anew by the spread of technology and its ability to equip new writers of an even greater variety of abilities and expressions. In his broadcast series *Do You Speak American?* from 2005, Robert MacNeil has this exchange with *New York* magazine writer John Simon, an immigrant from what was then called Yugoslavia who admires Standard English as the English language at its best:

> MACNEIL: How would you describe the state of our language today?
> SIMON: Unhealthy, poor, sad, depressing, um, and probably fairly hopeless.[6]

Simon speaks for many North Americans. To them, the hope is that a more robust curriculum of English grammar would help English speakers to be more structured and elegant in their speaking and writing. Other dialects, in this view, are a threat. In the late 1990s, heated controversy surrounded a resolution calling for the teaching of African-American Vernacular English (AAVE), or so-called "ebonics," in public schools in Oakland, California. While some of the resulting public outrage stemmed from the Oakland school board's decision to ask that AAVE be recognized as its own language, much of it resulted from prejudice that that AAVE was an inferior form of English. In some of the harshest criticism of the school board's resolution, AAVE was in turn called "mutant," "lazy," "defective," "ungrammatical," or "broken English."[7]

Whether or not the Oakland school board's resolution was the right proposal, and the best way to propose it, sociolinguists know two important truths about AAVE: first, it is syntactically and phonologi-

---

5. For treatment of how minority groups establish their identity through linguistic reconstruction, or alternate linguistic usage, see Pasquale, Ferwerda and Pearson (2008) for theoretical foundations and Pasquale, Pearson, and Ferwerda (2008) for examples of linguistic reconstruction from Chicano English.

6. *Do You Speak American?* Host Robert MacNeil.

7. Linguistic Society of America, "LSA Resolution on the Oakland 'Ebonics' Issue."

cally sophisticated,[8] and second, it can help students for whom AAVE is their natural dialect to learn both Standard English and AAVE in the classroom, comparing and contrasting their respective features and the settings in which they would be expected.[9]

In fact, any teacher of Standard English could benefit from an approach that emphasizes that Standard English is a dialect, among other dialects. This dialect is important and useful, and is expected in formal settings, especially in business, government, and education. Poorly executed Standard English is indeed a problem in these environments, and education should properly prepare students to use Standard English well when communicating in these settings. However, the Standard English dialect is not inherently superior to others; it is merely what has been agreed upon by socialization and tradition. And in fact, this dialect is actually out of place in many settings, such as the home. If we try to use Standard English with family members or others we feel close to, we will sound impersonal and distant. So we must switch to another dialect. We usually do this quite naturally, the same way we wear different clothes to a wedding, an office, a living room, or a backyard garden. We adapt to the context.

One concluding observation about AAVE is that speakers of a variety of dialects, including many speakers of Standard English, admire AAVE as especially sincere, expressive, rhythmic, and even poetic.[10] Whether or not this is a romanticized view of AAVE, it is important to note that even in this tacit admiration lies an acknowledgment that linguistic diversity can be beautiful and that enforced monotony would deprive us of the full range of expression within a language.

And so, although AAVE is significantly different from slang, it may be worth concluding by looking at both slang and language play as two important ways in which linguistic monotony is resisted and humans' creative linguistic impulses are affirmed.

---

8. For a good overview of the syntax and phonology of AAVE, see Fought, *Language and Ethnicity*, 47–51.

9. For a good reference on the pedagogy and method of this approach, see Wheeler, *Code-Switching: Teaching Standard English in Urban Classrooms*.

10. Fought, *Language and Ethnicity*, 54.

"LANGUAGE WITH ITS SLEEVES ROLLED UP"

If standardization is seen as the pure form of a language to which all language must conform, then one clear enemy of the health of a language is slang, or informal words and pronunciations. As long as there have been schools, there have been alternate vocabularies and pronunciations in the form of slang, and these alternates have been seen as subversive. Indeed, much slang revels in its defiance of acceptable norms—so much so that the examples included below will notably omit the vulgarity that seems central to slang. (The below roundup will also omit the innumerable slang words for intoxication, whose sheer proliferation may indicate slang's fascination with defying social propriety.)

Slang is organic; it's the language that thrives outside the halls of power and starched collars of formal society. "Slang is a colourful, alternative vocabulary," says the *Oxford Dictionary of Modern Slang*. "It bristles with humour, vituperation, prejudice, informality: the slang of English is English with its sleeves rolled up, its shirt-tails dangling, and its shoes covered in mud."[11] Unlike standard English, with rigid rules and top-down imposition, slang is grass-roots, it's non-prescribed; you can't trace where it came from and where it's going. For these very reasons, slang usually has much greater potential to influence a language—even as, ironically, slang so resists the mainstream and embraces its contrarian character that it fears its own linguistic influence.

And yet, slang is constantly proclaimed to be a danger to a language. According to some, slang is often lazy, vulgar, or cynical—and threatens to lower the quality of a society's language (if not social health in general!) This accusation has been made for centuries, and it's almost always wrong. As Edwin Battistella writes, "The argument that slang 'robs the language' and 'preys on vocabulary' misses the point that the living language is a marketplace of ideas, nuances, and images."[12]

Indeed, slang is language at its liveliest and most earnest—and arguably, its most healthy. "Slang," wrote Walt Whitman, "is an attempt of common humanity to escape from bald literalism, and express itself illimitably."[13] To fear slang, then, is to fear poetry.

---

11. *Stone the Crows: The Oxford Dictionary of Modern Slang*, ix.
12. Battistella, *Bad Language*, 89.
13. Whitman, "Slang in America."

Indeed, it may be slang's ambition to defy propriety that makes it so creative. Two linguists in *American Speech* pick up on this as they attempt to move toward a technical linguistic definition of slang:

> There is, however, an indispensible use for the term SLANG to name a body of lexemes that are distinct from standard English, jargon, and all other kinds of informal uses such as regionalisms and colloquialisms and which are identifiable primarily by the intent (or perceived intent) of the speaker or writer to break with established linguistic convention.[14]

This is not to say that all slang is beautiful or poetic. As noted above, much slang is vulgar, derogatory, and dehumanizing. As we saw in chapter 1, our linguistic creativity gives us the ability to speak beauty into the chaos or speak chaos into the beauty, and slang can certainly do both. But to assume slang only represents the worst aspects of language is to miss a world of creativity.

Consider a small sampling of slang from the *Oxford Dictionary of Modern Slang*. A short list shows that the line between slang, idiom, and metaphor is thin and sometimes seemingly invisible. But in essence slang is language on the loose.

alley, right up—to be suited or congenial to a person.

clobber—to defeat heavily.

front burner, on the—of an issue, etc. in the state of being actively or urgently considered; in the forefront of attention.

loon—a crazy person; a simpleton.

wrap, to wrap up—to be quiet, to stop talking.

Adhering strictly to Standard English and conventional usage of words such as these would allow for no double meanings, no new meanings, no creative re-purposing of words and metaphors to create a new rhetorical effect. We can celebrate the creativity behind this kind of expression, and encourage it as a way of imagining new linguistic possibilities.

---

14. Dumas and Lighter, "Is *Slang* a Word for Linguists?" 5–17.

LANGUAGE AT PLAY

Ask any lifelong fan of puns, or plays on the double meanings of words, and they'll tell you their craft is unappreciated. Ask any family member of a lifelong fan of puns, and they may roll their eyes and consider a fondness for puns an affliction.

This look at puns and other forms of language play is not primarily intended to defend pun lovers, convince pun haters, or even to entertain readers. The point is to appreciate creativity in language as one essential form of our use of language, to recognize that artistic and open-ended uses of language should be appreciated alongside purely functional uses of language, and ultimately to see that creativity in language is yet another way, and an important way, in which we bear the image of God in our use of language.

To get the feel for language play, sample some puns from the repository at www.punoftheday.com. Although it ruins a joke to explain it, notes are included here about the idioms or homonyms at work in these examples:

> *I used to have a fear of hurdles, but I got over it.*
> (Plays on the double meaning of "over it" as an idiom for meaning something no longer bothers the speaker.)
>
> *He didn't tell his mother that he ate some glue. His lips were sealed.*
> (Plays on the idiom "lips were sealed" to mean he will not divulge a secret.)
>
> *When the waiter spilled a drink on his shirt, he said, "This one is on me."*
> (Plays on the idiom "on me" meaning the speaker will pay for it.)
>
> *Having children is a heir raising experience.*
> (Plays on the similar sound of "hair" and "heir.")
>
> *He drove his expensive car into a tree and found out how the Mercedes bends.*
> (Plays on the similar sound of "bends" and "Benz" in the brand name "Mercedes Benz.")

"About two-thirds of the jokes in a typical collection rely on language play, and the vast majority of these involve puns of some kind," writes David Crystal in *Language Play*.[15] He calls for puns and language play to

---

15. Crystal, *Language Play*, 1.

be appreciated—if not always enjoyed or laughed at—and, at some level, to be taken seriously.

> [T]he playful (or 'ludic') function of language is important for our appreciation of language as a whole. Ludic language has traditionally been a badly neglected subject of linguistic enquiry—at best treated as a topic of marginal interest, at worst never mentioned at all. Yet it should be at the heart of any thinking we do about linguistic issues.

And, we might add, at the heart of any thinking we do about a Christian perspective on language. James Vanden Bosch writes about the importance of language play in Christian education about language, but we could extend his comments to apply to all Christian linguistic study.[16]

> Christian education must emphasize the importance of language play, both in language learning and in everyday life, in ordinary and in artistic forms of expression. Playfulness with language should be a recognizable feature of student life, in the curriculum, in the classroom, and in the larger world of schooling.... Learning to capitalize on the human creativity and playfulness that comes naturally with language may be one of the ways to help our students experience the great joy of having this gift. It may make our students less resistant, less insecure about their communication skills, less sullen in relationship to the authority of experts, and more joyful in the making and keeping of promises. Putting these assumptions to work, allowing these dispositions to be actualized in the classroom and beyond, could do a great deal to humanize and Christianize the students we work with, the schools that they learn in, and the societies in which these students take their place.[17]

One reason Christians should be especially attuned to creativity and play in language is that God's revealed Word is full of such expression. As we saw in the last chapter, when the Psalmist uses poetic imagery for washing, and Hebrews uses extensive alliteration, it shows that the God of language and of humanity revels in the creative use and playful ambiguity of language, rather than resorting to a purely functional and mechanical approach to language.

---

16. For more on language play in education, see Cook, *Language Play, Language Learning*.

17. Vanden Bosch, "Language Power, Language Play, and Promises to Keep."

We also examined how limiting the translatability of some of the words and wording of Scripture is. Since language play relies on sounds and idioms inherent in one language, something linguistic is inevitably lost when an attempt is made to translate it into another language. While this chapter has focused mostly on English examples, all languages have capacity for creativity and play, and for unique treasures, creations, and jokes that are possible only in that language.

God is a creative God; God revels in delight, in beauty, in something that was crafted or created. The more we resort to a view of language as merely a way to achieve a goal (proving a point, making the sale, winning votes, ordering a pizza), and neglect these other dimensions of language, we have a narrow view of language, and by extension, a narrow view of the God behind it.

8

Go Into All the World

Transformed Linguistic Communities

WE HAVE SEEN THAT human beings were created in the image of a communicating God, created to use linguistic symbols to communicate meaning. The effects of sin lead us to miscommunicate, both deliberately and unintentionally, perpetuating our pride, frustration, and helplessness. Christ's work of redemption includes the realm of linguistic communication: God restores us to loving and life-giving language use and variety. We have also seen that linguistic diversity is nothing less than a response to the call of Scripture, from Babel to Pentecost to the heavenly church in Revelation "of every tribe and tongue." We argue that Christians must be consistent with this vision by embracing and living out multilingual and multidialectal diversity. Christians can embrace and encourage the multilingual gifts of their friends and neighbors, use multiple languages themselves, and seek greater cross-cultural understanding through language.

If Christians passionately follow this call to linguistic diversity, communities can be transformed. This can start at the church level and can spread into surrounding neighborhoods and communities. Our loving response to others and their language is crucial. We have seen how language and dialect is intrinsically linked to one's identity. By affirming that God delights in worship that is diverse and multilingual and multidialectal, we welcome all to join in that celebration. If churches take these actions, there is an element of risk. There may be instances of confusion and anxiety in not understanding everything completely, that is, to get outside of a comfort zone. However, following a path of obedience is not always comfortable or easy, but the results can change their churches and communities for the better. So what do these churches look like? What are the characteristics of churches that have a biblical vision for language in society? We will offer a few case studies to show that any church—large or small, urban, suburban, or rural—can embrace linguistic diversity.

EXAMPLES OF TRANSFORMED LINGUISTIC COMMUNITIES

Developing a Cross-Cultural "Mission"

One of the most important characteristics of churches that exemplify linguistic diversity is their passion to define themselves by it. They understand that reaching out cross-culturally is not just for the "mission field." This vision is developed and owned by the church at the level of defining their church's mission statement: that is, how they are going to engage their world for Christ. If there is not a "buy-in" from the church at large, such risk-taking will fail to become a defining feature of the church.

Some churches have excelled at this and have made big adjustments to the way they approach life as a church. For example, some churches have dropped more exclusionary denominational labels in favor of broader ones such as including "International" or "All Nations" in their names. A change in mission can be announced loud and clear through a name change such as this. The factor that seems to distinguish churches who do this successfully is that it becomes a part of the whole church culture and is not relegated to the fringe. Many churches offer outreach ministries such as English as a Second Language classes or food pantries. However, these are often manned by a few people and do not become a defining characteristic of the whole church.

If a church wishes to be a part of transforming its community, it must agree on a mission statement that reflects the value of linguistic diversity and the desire to have a church that mirrors God's plan for diversity and creativity. So the first step is that churches must look inward to see who they are and what God wants them to become, that is, churches that embrace this call for linguistic hospitality.

A Heterogeneous, Not Homogeneous, Linguistic Community in Worship

Churches that embrace linguistic diversity in worship and large group gatherings see success in creating an environment that is welcoming and hospitable. The church must seek ways to integrate other languages into its worship rituals and practices. We mentioned one aspect is using a wide variety of Bible translations in personal and corporate worship. This includes a deeper knowledge of the original Hebrew and Greek languages that starts at the pastoral level, but is spread to the whole church through linguistic features being brought out in sermons and Bible studies that will result in enriching the congregation. Another key point is for churches to anticipate non-English speaking visitors who will eventually become members integrated into the church. A church should have Bibles available in other languages and easier-to-read English versions such as the New International Readers Version (NIrV), which is geared for a 3rd grade reading level. Also, pastors can prepare sermon outlines and handouts that can define hard terminology.[1]

The church's celebration of diversity should also include the choice of music used, both in style and language. A church can use music that the church is familiar with, but have it sung in another language. A translation could be shown on a screen behind the musicians so that the congregation can follow along and understand. The point is to engage in worship practices that celebrate linguistic diversity. Churches can also include times of prayer in various languages. It is a special blessing to hear people praise God in several languages and to understand that we are all bound together by one God. It gives the church a better perspective of the world-wide universal church. The second step, then, in transforming a church is to look outward, and anticipate and prepare for a linguistically diverse congregation. Churches must be prepared to show linguistic hospitality.

Differences Large and Small

There will be differences in execution and opportunities depending on the size and resources of the church. For example, a large church may have the means to hire a diverse pastoral staff. When people visit the church and see someone like them "up front" and in a position of leadership, it does help make a connection between the visitor and the church. A large church may also be able to be engaged in many outreach ministries. They may have the space and personnel necessary to offer programs

---

1. This could also be useful for their English speaking congregation for that matter. A good source for simplified theological terms can be found in Eby, Lyon, and Truesdale, *Dictionary of the Bible & Christian Doctrine in Everyday English*.

such as a food or clothes pantry, ESL classes, financial planning courses, sports leagues, etc. A church may also have the budget to expand their church library to include books written in a variety of languages.

However, small churches with limited budgets can also effectively relate to a diverse culture. They may have a diverse volunteer staff that would be a part of worship teams or teaching classes. They may be able to offer a limited number of outreach programs, or put all of their energy into one such as offering an ESL class. A church library can be stocked and expanded through donations from parishioners or ministries.

CASE STUDIES

The following examples are based on actual churches we have ministered in or have provided consultation for. These are examples of some "best practices" that we have observed. You will see that there is not a one-size-fits-all approach, but a general conviction from these churches that they must reach out to a diverse world in need around them.

Small Rural Church

A small church recognized that there was, in fact, diversity even in their remote rural context. Every year migrant farmers came to work the vast orchards and farms in the surrounding town and county. The church felt an obligation to adopt a mission statement that recognized that these workers were made in God's image and therefore would share and minister to their needs, both physical and spiritual. At first they guessed at what the farmers and their families needed—for example offering English as a Second Language classes and hosting a food pantry at church. The food pantry was well-used, but the ESL classes were not well-attended. In fact, the time the classes were held was not at all convenient for the workers themselves due to their work schedule. The church decided to ask the farmers and their hosts how the church could best minister to them. ESL classes were desired, but they needed them offered at the farm (due to lack of transportation) and later in the evening (in this case, at 10:00 p.m.). This act of humility and willingness to serve the farmers was well received and the classes were well-attended. The church sought to build connections beyond those made by the English teachers. They decided that in order to bring the church family and the migrant farmers together, they would host a harvest party in the fall at the church to celebrate the end of a year and to build relationships. The church was then pondering the next steps they could take. One idea was having a worship service together using both Spanish and English hymns and choruses. Another was to host a Bible study in Spanish at church on Sunday afternoons. The church began to realize that this relationship would be a long-term commitment and they would relish the chance to serve the world at their doorstep.

Small Suburban Church

This church found itself surrounded by many other larger churches in close proximity. The church went through a process of deciding whether or not to remain open as a congregation or to define their mission in a way to meet a need in the community. This small congregation decided that, in fact, the church would remain open and have at its core the mission to reach its diverse community for Christ. The other larger churches in the area were rather homogenous, and none offered ESL classes or other services to meet needs of non-English speaking immigrants in town. They wondered how they were going to actually get in contact with ESL students so as to start making these connections. One solution was to serve as volunteers at the adult education ESL program run through their local public school system. Through this program, they offered to serve as conversation partners and to fill in any roles needed by being faithful volunteers. They asked permission from the school administrator to invite students to the church for a Sunday ESL class. That was the opening they needed to continue to build into students' lives. They offered a Sunday morning ESL class during the Sunday school hour and then they concluded with a meal attended by most of the church members. It was a very effective way to build relationships among students and church members. One of the next steps the church was pondering was how to integrate their international members into the life of the church. Some ideas considered were to offer multilingual services, including using music in alternate languages. They also discussed providing easy English outlines of the sermon notes to help non-native English speakers to follow along.

Over time the number of ESL students that came to Christ nearly outnumbered the original congregation itself. It was satisfying to the church to see men and women return to their home countries as believers and "missionaries," even though as a church they had very little funding to support traditional missionaries. The members of this small suburban church were excited that they were able to engage in the global missions enterprise without having to leave their city.

Medium-Sized Urban Church

In this case a healthy mid-sized church decided to do something radical. They decided to embrace whole-heartedly the mission to reach the diverse community around them. In fact, they decided to be identified with that very mission by discarding their denominational label from their church name and replacing it with "International Church." They intentionally sought to make connections with local immigrant and refugee communities in their city to see how they could help. One of the results was the formation of Haitian and Vietnamese congregations that also met in their building. The church welcomed these congregations as part of their "family" and sought to work with them to forge deeper ties of fellowship and shared mission. This was done through hosting multilingual worship services in which ministry leaders from all three groups shared with the combined group (using interpreters during the service) and enjoying a multilingual praise and worship time. An all-church meal also was common and folk enjoyed tasting food from different cultures.

The church also sought to provide a welcoming environment to visitors of all cultures. They wanted to reach people not merely from international communities, but specifically from diverse populations in their own community. Greeters were trained to be able to be multilingual in phrases such as "welcome" and "Can I help you?" The church also had multilingual directional signs in the building and was decorated with flags and artifacts from various countries.

One way the church also served the community was to offer ESL classes. They offered courses during the day twice a week and in the evening once a week. Childcare was also offered at each class time. This allowed mothers with young children to benefit from the classes. The frequency of the courses also allowed for more opportunity for students to take courses.

The idea of ministering to a multicultural community helped give life and meaning to a church that at one time was worried that it spent too much time looking inward. This church recognized a world in need and acted in a way to bring Christ's love to them.

Large Suburban Church

There are a few examples of large suburban churches that we can illustrate. But at least one case involves a church located in a city that was home to a large state university. This church established an extensive ESL program that met twice a week in the evenings. This program had over 100 students and had various levels from advanced (to help the international students with academic English) to low beginner (for spouses or other recent immigrants). The church had resources to provide space and materials for an excellent educational program. Over time the church was able to hire a pastor directly related to international ministries and worked to build a small congregation of international members that would meet within the church building.

One down side to having a large church is that even though the international ministries program was quite extensive, it still had a hard time preventing marginalization from the larger church function. With so many ministries and so many members, it was hard for the church as a whole to identify with the cross-cultural mission.

Another large church attempted a different plan to reach its diverse community. They partnered with a local refugee services organization and "adopted" a people group. They made it a goal to help all new refugees from one particular country, in this case, Haiti. A church family or families would be matched up with each new refugee family, and the church family would provide rides, meals, and perhaps informal English tutoring. This built strong bonds among the families and was quite effective.

The church also wanted to reach the internationals in the community but felt that they were too far out in the suburbs to have direct impact due to transportation issues. They planted a church and gave it a title containing the phrase "International Fellowship." This was planted in a local community center near diverse neighborhoods. People from the congregation volunteered at the weekly Saturday outreach and fellowship times. It was a way for the church to minister in a smaller, more intimate setting. In all of these situations there wasn't one particular way that worked for all. Each church sought effective ways to reach those in their community from around the world.

CONCLUSION

Christian communities living out the gospel authentically must resist the world's ways of looking at language conformity, national loyalty, class superiority, and other marks of sin in human linguistic communication. A community transformed through Christ will be marked in part by its transformed vision for language as a gift from God, and will see itself as called out from the world to model a new way of appreciating and using language in society that anticipates the heavenly gathering of every tribe and tongue.

Bibliography

Alter, Robert. *The Book of Psalms: A Translation With Commentary*. New York: Norton, 2007. 180.
Atkins, J. D. C. *Annual Report of the Federal Commissioner of Indian Affairs 1887*. Excerpted in *Language Loyalties: A Source book on the Official English Controversy*, edited by J. Crawford. Chicago: University of Chicago Press, 1992.
Ayto, John, and John Simpson. *Stone the Crows: The Oxford Dictionary of Modern Slang*. 2nd ed. New York: Oxford University Press, 2008.
Bamford, K. W., and D. T. Mizokawa. "Additive-Bilingual (Immersion) Education: Cognitive and Language Development." *Language Learning* 41 (1991) 413-29.
Battistella, Edwin. *Bad Language: Are Some Words Better Than Others?* New York: Oxford University Press, 2005.
Bialystok, E. "Metalinguistic Aspects of Bilingual Processing." *Annual Review of Applied Linguistics* 21 (2001) 169-81.
Bialystok, E., and K. Hakuta. "Confounded Age: Linguistic and Cognitive Factors in Age Differences for Second Language Acquisition." In *Second Language Acquisition and the Critical Period Hypothesis*, edited by D. Birdsong, 161-81. Mahweh, NJ: Lawrence Erlbaum.
Bierma, Nathan L. K. *Bringing Heaven Down to Earth: Connecting This Life to the Next*. Phillipsburg, NJ: P. & R., 2005.
———. "The Words of the Word." *Books & Culture* (April 2005). Online: http://www.booksandculture.com/articles/webexclusives/2005/April/050418.html.
Bikales, Gerda. "The Treaty of Guadaloupe-Hidalgo: Truth and Consequences." *The Social Contract* 5 (1994) 19-20.
Blue Letter Bible. "Dictionary and Word Search for *Logos (Strong's 3056)*." Blue Letter Bible. 1996-2010. Online: http://www.blueletterbible.org/lang/lexicon/lexicon.cfm?Strongs=G3056&t=KJV.
Bruggemann, Walter. *Genesis: Interpretation, A Bible Commentary for Teaching and Preaching*. Atlanta: John Knox, 1982.
Canagarajah, Suresh. *Resisting Linguistic Imperialism in English Teaching*. Oxford: Oxford University Press, 1999.
Carroll, Bret E. *The Routledge Historical Atlas of Religion in America*. New York: Routledge, 2000.
Carroll R., M. Daniel. *Christians at the Border: Immigration, the Church, and the Bible*. Grand Rapids: Baker Academic, 2008.
Chomsky, Noam. *Aspects of the Theory of Syntax*. Cambridge: MIT Press, 1965.
Cook, Guy. *Language Play, Language Learning*. New York: Oxford University Press, 2000.
Crystal, David. *The Fight for English: How Language Pundits Ate, Shot, and Left*. New York: Oxford University Press, 2006.

———. *Language Play*. Chicago: University of Chicago Press, 2001.
Daniels, Roger. *Coming to America: A History of Immigration and Ethnicity in American Life*. New York: HarperCollins, 2002.
Derr, Nancy. "The Babel Proclamation." *The Palimpsest* 60 (1979) 100–15.
Desmond, Humphrey Joseph. *The Know-Nothing Party: A Sketch*. Washington: New Century, 1904.
Do You Speak American? Host Robert MacNeil. PBS. WNET, New York, January 5, 2005. Online: http://www.pbs.org/speak/transcripts/1.html.
Dumas, Bethany K., and Jonathan Lighter. "Is *Slang* a Word for Linguists?" *American Speech* 53 (1978) 5–17.
Eby, J. Wesley, George Lyons, and Albert Truesdale. *Dictionary of the Bible & Christian Doctrine in Everyday English*. Kansas City, MO: Beacon Hill, 2004.
Edmonston, Barry. *Statistics on U.S. Immigration: An Assessment of Data Needs for Future Research*. Washington, DC: National Academy, 1996.
Emerson, Michael O. *People of the Dream: Multiracial Congregations in the United States*. Princeton: Princeton University Press, 2006.
Emerson, Michael O., and Christian Smith. *Divided by Faith: Evangelical Religion and the Problem of Race in America*. Oxford: Oxford University Press, 2000.
Fee, Gordon, and Mark Strauss. *How to Choose a Translation for All Its Worth: A Guide to Understanding and Using Bible Versions*. Grand Rapids: Zondervan, 2007.
Fillmore, Lily Wong. "What Happens When Languages Are Lost? An Essay on Language Assimilation and Cultural Identity. In *Social Interaction, Social Context, and Language: Essays in Honor of Susan Ervin-Tripp*, edited by Dan I. Slobin et al. Mahwah, NJ: Lawrence Erlbaum, 1996.
Flom, George Tobias. *A History of Norwegian Immigration to the United States*. Cedar Rapids, IA: Torch, 1909.
Fought, Carmen. *Chicano English in Context*. New York: Palgrave Macmillan. 2003.
———. *Language and Ethnicity*. New York: Cambridge University Press, 2006.
Franz, Gordon. "Nahum and Nineveh." *Associates for Biblical Research* (6 Sept. 2006). Online: http://www.biblearchaeology.org/post/2006/09/06/Nahum-and-Nineveh.aspx.
———. "Nahum, Nineveh and Those Nasty Assyrians." *Associates for Biblical Research* (28 May 2009). Online: http://www.biblearchaeology.org/post/2009/05/28/Nahum 2c-Nineveh-and-Those-Nasty-Assyrians.aspx.
Haugen, Einer. *The Norwegian Language in America: A Study in Bilingual Behavior*. Bloomington: Indiana University Press, 1969.
Hoffmeier, James K. *The Immigration Crisis: Immigrants, Aliens, and the Bible*. Wheaton, IL: Crossway, 2009.
Kenny, Kevin. *The American Irish: A History*. New York: Pearson Longman, 2000.
King, Martin Luther. *A Testament of Hope: The Essential Writings and Speeches of Martin Luther King*. Edited by James Melvin Washington. New York: Harper Collins, 1986.
King, Kendallm, and Lyn Fogle, "Raising Bilingual Children: Parental Concerns and Current Research." *CAL Digest*, April 2006.
Krish, John, and Peter Sykes, directors. *Jesus*. Inspirational Films. 1979
Lenneberg, Eric H. *Biological Foundations of Language*. New York: Wiley, 1967.
Lewis, M. Paul, editor. *Ethnologue: Languages of the World*. 16th ed. Dallas, TX: SIL International, 2009.

Bibliography

Long, Thomas. *Hebrews (Interpretation, a Bible Commentary for Teaching and Preaching)*. Westminster John Knox, 1997.

"LSA Resolution on the Oakland 'Ebonics' Issue." Language Society of America (January 3, 1997). Online: http://www.lsadc.org/info/lsa-res-ebonics.cfm.

McCarthy, Suzanne. "hyssop." *Better Bibles Blog* (11 May 2008). Online: http://betterbibles.com/2008/05/11/hyssop/.

Meier, Samuel. *Themes and Transformations in Old Testament Prophecy*. Downers Grove, IL: InterVarsity, 2009.

Norton, Bonny. *Identity and Language Learning: Gender, Ethnicity and Educational Change*. New: Longman, 2000.

Okkema, Bruce, and Lois Tverberg. *Listening to the Language of the Bible*. En-Gedi Resource Center, 2004.

Pasquale, Michael, Gillian Ferwerda, and Amber Pearson. "Voicing Identity in Chicano English." *Academic Exchange Quarterly* (Winter 2008).

Pasquale, Michael, Amber Pearson, and Gillian Ferwerda. "Chicano English as Linguistic Reconstruction." In *Selected Proceedings from the 2007 MITESOL Conference*, edited by C. Pearson, K. Losey, and N. Caplan. Eastern Michigan University, 2008.

Peterson, Eugene H. *Subversive Spirituality*. Grand Rapids: Eerdmans, 1994.

Porterfield, Jason. *The Homestead Act of 1862*. New York: Rosen, 2005.

"Randall Dale Adams." *Center on Wrongful Convictions*. Online: http://www.law.northwestern.edu/wrongfulconvictions/exonerations/txAdamsSummary.html.

Rendsburg, Gary. "Wordplay in Biblical Hebrew: An Eclectic Collection." In *Puns and Pundits: Word Play in the Hebrew Bible and Ancient Near Eastern Literature*, edited by Noegel, Scott, 137–62. Capital Decisions, 2000.

Rienstra, Debra, and Ron Rienstra. *Worship Words: Discipling Language for Faithful Ministry*. Grand Rapids: Baker, 2009.

Roosevelt, Theodore. *Works*. New York: Scribners, 1926.

Schultze, Quentin. *Communicating for Life: Christian Stewardship in Community and Media*. Grand Rapids: Baker, 2000.

Seerveld, Calvin. *Voicing God's Psalms*. Grand Rapids: Eerdmans, 2005.

Shannon, William V. *The American Irish*. New York: MacMillan, 1963.

Smith, David. "What Hope after Babel? Diversity and Community in Genesis 11, Exodus 1, Zephaniah 3, and Acts 2." *Horizons in Biblical Theology* 18 (1996) 169–91.

Smith, David I., and Barbara Carvill. *The Gift of the Stranger: Faith, Hospitality, and Foreign Language Learning*. Grand Rapids: Eerdmans, 2000.

Smith, James P., and Barry Edmonston. *The New Americans: Economic, Demographic, and Fiscal Effects of Immigration*. Washington, DC: National Academy, 1997.

The SAT College Board. *College-bound Seniors: A Profile of SAT Program Test Takers*. College Entrance Examination Board, 2003. Online: www.collegeboard.com.

Thernstrom, Stephan. *Harvard Encyclopedia of American Ethnic Groups*. Cambridge: Harvard University Press, 1980.

Tomasi, Silvano M. *Piety and Power: The Role of Italian (Catholic and Protestant) Parishes in the New York Metropolitan Area: 1880–1930*. New York: Center for Migration Studies, 1975.

Tucker, G. Richard, "Global Perspective on Bilingualism and Bilingual Education." *CAL Digest*, August 1999.

United States Census Data 2000. Online: http://www.census.gov/main/www/cen2000.html.

Vanden Bosch, James. "Language Power, Language Play, and Promises to Keep: Language and the Image of God." International Association for the Promotion of Christian Higher Education, Moscow, August 2005.

Walton, John H., and Victor H. Matthews. *The IVP Bible Background Commentary: Genesis-Deuteronomy.* Downers Grove: InterVarsity, 1997.

Webb, Stephen. *Divine Voice: Christian Proclamation and the Theology of Sound.* Grand Rapids: Brazos, 2004.

Wheeler, Rebecca S. *Code-Switching: Teaching Standard English in Urban Classrooms.* Urbana, IL: National Council of Teachers of English, 2006.

Whitman, Walt. "Slang in America." 1892. Online: http://www.bartleby.com/229/5009.html.

Witherington, Ben, III. *Grace in Galatia: A Commentary on St. Paul's Letter to the Galatians.* Grand Rapids: Eerdmans, 1998.

———. *Letters and Homilies for Jewish Christians: A Socio-Rhetorical Commentary on Hebrews, James, and Jude.* Downers Grove, IL: InterVarsity Academic, 2007

Zimmer, Benjamin. "Ma Ferguson, the Apocryphal Know-nothing." *Language Log* (26 April 2006). Online: http://itre.cis.upenn.edu/~myl/languagelog/archives/003084.html.

www.ingramcontent.com/pod-product-compliance
Lightning Source LLC
Chambersburg PA
CBHW070936160426
43193CB00011B/1711